THE INTEGRITY OF LOVE

Carmen O'Connor

First published and distributed from the UK in 2019
by Carmen O'Connor, self-publishing author

ISBN 978 1 9993722 1 7

(eBook ISBN 978 1 9993722 0 0)

www.theintegrityoflove.com

About the Author

Carmen O'Connor is a human being navigating through life as best she can – just like everyone else. Having experienced a traumatic family environment growing up, she went on to work in the corporate world, but retrained and became a complementary therapist in 2000, and has worked with individuals as well as groups. She chose to write this book having journeyed through a lot of inner healing work herself, but also, through her complementary therapy training and work with clients, she felt the need to share her experiences in the hope that it will help others shorten their healing journey, and contribute to lifting the energy vibration of the earth through people's increased connection to consciousness and the true nature and *Integrity of Love.*

She asks the readers to challenge themselves through perceptive questioning, without judgement, but merely to help them connect more into consciousness and, in doing so, contribute to increasing the flow of the true nature and *Integrity of Love* within and around them.

It is also an invitation for the reader to align their actions with the natural compassion and *Love* residing in their heart and join a collective force and energy, for the sake of the reader, their families and friends, and future generations. In other words, the planet and all within and beyond it.

Gratitude

This book has been 49 years in the making and my life's work. I say this with a smile of course.

While writing this book I have been overwhelmed by the amount of mental and emotional pain I have actually endured. Dealing with it in separate scenarios over 49 years is probably why I am still alive today, but quite frankly gathered together in one place, it stuns me that I have survived it and am out the other side. I am grateful, and particularly so, that I followed my intuition and continued battling through the storm of my life to a place of vast yet simple peace and happiness. I now stand strong in my shoes, I can feel the Love in my heart and can acknowledge my strength and beingness. I am the essence I am in every aspect I am, and ever determined to show how compassion for self and others and the true nature and Integrity of Love will always win through in the end. Life is life and will probably always throw us curve balls, but it's how we catch them, swerve them and let them go that is key. Healing is possible.

During the journey known as my human life, I have had the deep privilege of meeting so many wonderfully kind-hearted people, generous of spirit and soul, and some extra-special beings who have guided me so beautifully during the healing journey. I'd like to thank you, each and every one for coming onto my path or passing me on it, for helping me on the way, as it continues each day of course, and in a way for contributing to this book through me. With my deep gratitude and Love for you all, and with my special thanks to:

Queen Evie for being the breath of joyous life that you are! Hampelé – the only one in the world. Andy Brown – not only for the lamp post sketch but for so much more. Noonie and G – for your acceptance of the whole of me; you are both so very special together and to me and Evie. Sash and G – for your continued love and support including financially when I was on my knees. Lou – you continue to inspire and shine brightly; thank you with all my heart. Glenda – you will always be my gentle rock; my deep gratitude and especially for all the 'hups' along the way. Michelle – for washing my towels and so much else.

John – for being THE most wonderfully decent, respectful and funny man and for enabling me to blossom. Lynda and Ian – for caring enough. Fenna – for helping me stay alive in the depths of darkness. My birth family – for sparking me to learn and heal so much. Stewart – for teaching me about Reiki and setting the bar so very high. Jeremy and Hans – for acknowledging and helping my left brain. Rachel and Meg – you rocked back then and you still rock now; please keep causing the revolution! Vinciane – for your homeopathic remedies and loving friendship. Gayle, Judith and Paula – for such a nurturing introduction to mindfulness. Jason Garner – you taught me to breathe again and to be gentle with myself while learning to accept my humanness and love myself in the process.

Kadampa friends, especially LJ – through your loving kindness you put a safe and honest arm around my shoulders and have opened my heart even further. Sadie – for getting it! T – for being able to trust in you. Carol – for all the years. Johanna, Jeremy Haas, and all at Challenge 22, Veganuary and Viva! – for opening my eyes to the vegan way. Meike – for encouraging me to write. Reiki – for cleansing and raising my vibration. Buddha's teachings – so many more of which I still wish to come to know. Dr Bach – for flooding my vibration with the virtues of plants. Jo Dunbar – for your exquisite grace and guidance through healing herbs. Etty – for connecting to the essence of this book and for respecting my words during the editing process. Iain Crockart – for your creative genius.

I also want to say a special thank you to all my clients, who over the years have allowed me to support them with my skills, while placing their mind, body and souls in my hands – it is a true privilege each and every time and I thank you for your deep trust. Each one of you is a jewel.

Lastly and absolutely by no means any less of course, my deep gratitude goes to the true nature and Integrity of Love itself for flowing round and through me, and onwards to all who may read this book. May we all be guided by the true nature and Integrity of Love, so we raise our vibration and support our planet in light, for the sake of ALL within it and beyond.

Dedication

I dedicate this book in a number of ways and although I make individual references, I write this dedication understanding that there is no separation, and all are connected and contained within it.

To all readers and those you cross paths with

By reading this book, you join a collective force or energy and contribute to raising the vibration of Integrity and Love within our planet and therefore beyond, simply by consciously connecting and melding with the true nature and Integrity of Love fully and in turn sharing this Love through your thoughts, actions and behaviours. Thank you.

To my goddaughter, Nell

My wish for you, Nell, is that you stay consciously connected to the flow of the true nature and Integrity of Love. You have a delightful spirit and my wish for you is to continue living from your authentic nature and your true essence, for it is gentle, loving, kind, funny, intelligent, quirky, defiantly sparky and wilful. You have great heart, my dear and sweet girl, and as you grow and blossom throughout the rest of your life, may you know consciously the true nature and Integrity of Love, so it may guide you and all those you meet. You will then have a truly peaceful and joyful life. May you come to know and instinctively refer to the phrase 'The Integrity of Love'.

To the animals

May you no longer suffer at the hands of unconscious humans. May we all awaken to the suffering we have caused you and particularly the huge scale of cruelty we have caused during the last 50 years. I have been and am continuously appalled at the cruelty the human species inflicts upon you, purely for the sake of their taste buds and greed on many differing levels. I also once did through simple ignorance of not making the connection, I am deeply sorry. Rest assured though, there is a movement working tirelessly and raising awareness for you. We are doing our very best to stop this hell in which you are forced to live and die, and in such heinous conditions and circumstances.

Contents

Introduction

I grew up in a created environment that included, but was not limited to, chaos, hate, jealousy, separation, cruelty, anger, and more. Yet mostly this was described to me as an environment of 'love'. This was not Love. I don't doubt many of these elements of life experience will touch almost each reader who will have experienced at least one of them if not more. These elements have been 'normalised', but they are not 'Love'.

This life I was born into was no mistake as far as I am concerned. It is leading me to unearthing deep Love and sharing in that, so I am neither bitter nor angry about it now. I *have* been, and hugely so along the way, but healing the inner pain is possible, through patience, time and by connecting more into consciousness. I will share with you my 'story' and what I have learned along the way in the hope that you too can heal any pain you may have within your being, particularly emotional and mental pain.

So I hold several reasons at my heart for choosing to write this book and invite you to:

- Awaken and connect to the true nature and Integrity of Love, which is what I will explain in this book.
- Come to know that healing is possible and gain insights from my 'story' which may help shorten your healing journey out of pain and into more peace and gentleness.
- Lessen the importance of 'I and me' to increase togetherness, due regard and cherishing of ALL life. Narcissism is destructive and dark and of late seems to have been on the rise, but as you will come to understand through this book, those behaviours will take us to darker places if we do not wake up to them now.
- SLOW DOWN, reduce greed and the wanting of 'stuff' so you can come more into the reality and flow at your heart centre. There is more in this flow than we can possibly imagine.
- Experience your essence and the relief that being in the space of your authentic beingness can provide.

- Align your actions with the compassion in your heart, for the sake of all living beings, future generations and the planet. We can individually and collectively raise our game as humans.

When I have run workshops and seminars I say 'cherry pick' from what I will share with you, some of it will resonate and if it doesn't then ignore it. It's the same in this book. Some of it will resonate, other parts of it may sound bonkers to you. Similarly, if you read things and you don't feel that part applies to you, there is no need to feel offence, you can simply read on. As the old saying goes: "If the cap doesn't fit, don't wear it." All I will say is if something irritates you, that is a really good indicator to look into your heart and see what potentially needs healing.

This is a book based on my own life experiences, my 'story' to date. I do not share this for cathartic reasons nor in a vengeful way at all as I have worked through a lot of this 'stuff' deeply over the years and it is now in the past, which is why I am now able to share it. So I share these experiences in good faith and in the deep hope that the true nature and Integrity of Love will lift us all even more to a higher energetic vibration – for the sake of all in equal measure.

As you read, you may feel judgements arising within you, particularly with regard to me and my family, or perhaps you identify with someone in your own circle and make judgements of them. I would simply ask that for now, you suspend any judgements on people, if you would be so kind. I will explain why in more depth later in the book. Neither, by the way, do I sit in judgement of anyone reading this book. That simply is not what I or this book are about, but I will ask questions of you throughout that may challenge you. They are asked so you can contemplate them from deep within your heart. They are asked so you can consider fleshing out the unhelpful behaviours we humans naturally fall into when we're not paying attention to where our bodyminds take us, and so that you can let the unhelpful behaviours go, if you so wish of course. That choice is yours though. I merely sit here sharing and shedding light on issues many of us may face at times in our lives and that I feel drawn to do something about.

'***Questions***' are for you to contemplate and '***Actions***' are for you to try if you wish. They will be indicated by ***Question*** and ***Action*** respectively. Remember, in each moment you have a choice in this, so ensure you are fully conscious when you ask yourself the questions and whether or not you wish to try the actions. Above all, be gentle with yourself in this process.

There are also pages at the back if you wish to make notes as you are reading and contemplating.

In the meantime, I repeat that you are not being judged in any way, shape or form so try not to judge yourself too much either. Neither am I judging myself nor those I have crossed paths with and include in this book. I have consciously chosen to share my 'story' with you and I write it all purely as a gift to anyone who reads it, as well as in support of this wondrous planet we have the good fortune and privilege to co-habit with each day.

Along my journey, I have been touched by Spirituality and by Dharma teachings and that is my path, although I realise I also still have much more to learn. I appreciate not everyone has been touched in this way so this is not saying I am right and you are wrong in your belief system. Not at all. We are all entitled to follow our chosen path, whether that has a label and deep teachings behind a symbol or not. However, I will occasionally touch on how Spirituality and Dharma have contributed to my coming to resonate with the true nature and Integrity of Love, but this is not in any way to say that is how it will be for you and nor am I making judgements if you do not follow a particular philosophy or faith. Please feel the freedom I offer you in saying this.

You will find the key to your portal or gateway to the Integrity of Love in the way that you do. Unlocking the flow of the true nature and Integrity of Love is what is important, and the path of getting there will probably be different for many of us. Buddhism is one of my guiding lights, so I cannot omit it from this book, but yours may be nature, God, the Universe, your depth and inner strength, or something else. So, feel free, for example, to switch the word Buddhism to whatever resonates for you if that will make it easier for you.

I also want to make it clear from the outset that I do not think I am perfect and by no means do I think I have all the answers and am some enlightened being – I don't profess to any of that. I have made plenty of mistakes along the way and will surely make many more in this human life I have the privilege to be living. In parts, I have simply coped in the best way I could, and as many of us do.

However, I want to share what I have experienced and observed as well as what I've learned in the hope it will inspire you the reader, to connect with the true nature and Integrity of Love as it flows through you in each moment, if you allow yourself to fully connect within. I am not referring to the attached, manipulated, messy form called 'love'. That isn't Love. Those types of behaviours, and others such as possessive jealousy, can in turn cause much pain. It's a deep connection to the true nature and Integrity of Love that inspires me in this life and I hope inspires you too.

Many within our planet, as well as Mother Earth herself, are suffering deeply at the hands of human behaviours, and yet it doesn't have to be this way if we just have the courage to trust a little more, open our hearts and become truly aware, tapping into our Integrity, our 'Wholeness' – which is a true translation of Integrity. My wish is not for anyone to be sorrowful about the path I'm treading either. I see this path as a means to clearing and cleansing my energy being through life experiences and that is my responsibility, so I'm grateful in many ways. Meantime, you can concentrate on giving yourself that great gift as well if you choose and hopefully more peace and Love can arise from within you too.

If you're up for learning about and experiencing more of the true nature and Integrity of Love in your life you may naturally have to go through a pain threshold of letting go of some old stuff or ways of thinking and being, and even perhaps let go of some people that you may once have been greatly attached to, but I promise you it will be worth it. Are you up for it? If so, read on…

Part 1:
Integrity and Love

Integrity

In my view, Integrity seems to have greatly reduced in society over the years, particularly in the UK where I live. Pictures on social media and stories on the news seem nothing short of barbaric at times.

Could it be that we can form a conscious group in raising Integrity in the form of moral decency and where we enable ourselves to come from wholeness? When darkness enters our behaviour, Integrity cannot be present, and so I often wonder how many people are aware of and will consciously understand what the true nature of Integrity is, so they can indeed abide by it?

While writing this book, I randomly asked people I know what 'Integrity' meant to them and I received replies like trustworthiness and being true to yourself and your own moral compass. I found these to be interesting replies, but for me these explanations seemed a couple of degrees out. However, one person (thanks, Janice) blew me away with…

Lead with the Heart Centre, asking self "What Would Love Do?"

For those new to these concepts, heart centre here refers to our spiritual heart and not the beating physical heart. My understanding is our heart centre is the energy centre within our being and located in the centre of the chest. It is the portal or gateway through which the true nature and Integrity of Love can flow.

Another explanation might be from a Buddhist perspective, where they know the heart centre to be where the mind resides, in other words, not in the head where many habitually think it is and we often live from, but again in the centre of the chest. When training to drop down with our awareness from the head and come into and from the heart centre, my personal experience in doing so is there is a vastness, more gentleness and kindness, less intensity, more peace, a calmness, less speed, more clarity, more understanding, less criticism and judgement, more natural strength. We can view our external and internal worlds as though our eyes are at our heart and we can feel or sense the world from here too.

Question: *Just out of curiosity – how many judgements popped up in your mind when I mentioned 'Buddhist' and did you do an internal eye roll? Once, I would have too, by the way! Anyway, if so, for what purpose did you allow this?*

Question: *Could you have simply suspended judgement and simply read the words from your heart centre, perhaps?*

Action: *If you made judgements, perhaps go back and re-read the above section from your heart without judgement, then simply contemplate how it would be for you by dropping down with your awareness into your heart centre.*

Action: *Contemplate your current circumstances from the heart centre and see how you view or experience it. Do you experience more gentleness and less judgement here, for example?*

Question: *How would it be to respond to life from this space?*

Action: *Try doing that, i.e. responding to life from the heart centre. Play with it when you remember to do so, starting with small things like smiling at someone, allowing your natural smile to come from your heart (not forcing falsely or performing), but also allow it to arise from your heart centre up to your face and smile from both. Notice any benefits or challenges.*

Question: *Does fear or pride arise, for example, and prevent you from doing this Action? Are you not in the habit of genuinely smiling at others?*

Question: *Could you perhaps trust that Love will see you through in this fearful moment of responding differently?*

Now let us look at 'Integrity' in some more detail. As I've already indicated, the word 'Integrity' has its roots in the meaning 'Wholeness' and the word 'Whole' links to the word 'Unharmed'. It also relates to 'Honesty' and 'Unity'.

When we observe our own behaviours, how often do we ask: "Am I in all honesty coming from a place of wholeness whereby no one including myself will be harmed to the best of my ability?" Don't worry – I think I know the answer to that! However, it's a good one to contemplate, so…

Action: *Observe and contemplate your behaviour like a hawk over the next while. Be really honest with yourself and simply question in your own mind: "From the honesty in my heart centre, when I do xyz, am I coming from a place of wholeness where there is no harm for myself and other beings – as much as possible?"*

You'll know if you are coming from Integrity because there will be no feeling of irritation or uncomfortable/awkward sensation in your heart centre or your being. Another way to know is if you notice a sense of deceit or darkness about your decisions or actions. It's like that feeling of telling a white lie or when you do something a bit sneaky and think no one was watching and you "got away with it". That cheeky mischief feeling perhaps. There is still a bit of discomfort in the heart centre if we are truly honest with ourselves. Your heart or being will tell you. It always does – if you notice. The key is then to adjust your actions and clear the slate, so Integrity can be present. I read the following quote online somewhere that seemingly came from C.S. Lewis, it's quite a good one to hold in mind.

"Integrity is doing the right thing even when no-one is watching."

With all our actions whether at work, within the family, with our pets, among friends, in doing business, and so on, we can ask our heart centre: "As much as possible, am I coming from a place of wholeness and for the benefit of all parties?"

In my humble opinion, and I'm pretty sure many of you would agree, if things are to improve here on planet earth, we must raise the Integrity stakes within human society because the levels of deceit and violence prevalent on our streets and in our communities has been too high for too long. We need to raise the level of Integrity present as a collective, but we can only do that by drawing a line in the sand and starting with ourselves.

Action: *Have some fun with this too, of course! Don't fall into the trap of being intensely serious with this stuff and give yourself the gift of not having to be perfect at it. Perhaps speak to your partner or friends about this and form a pact with them, for example the Integrity pact. If one of you is not fully coming from Integrity, then help each other do so. Not in a judgemental way, but in a compassionate, supportive and fun way. Then we can all begin to contribute to raising the levels of Integrity and joy around us. Governments, authorities and education establishments are not responsible for this within us, we as individuals are, as are those individuals working in such places, but as a collective force we are much more likely to see results happening more quickly.*

When we are asking "What would the true nature and Integrity of Love do?" we are asking "What would Wholeness, Honesty, Unity and Non-harmfulness do?" Our thoughts and actions will therefore not contain any harm – there is no element of harm nor deceit in the true nature of Integrity. Have courage, be brave, you will reap many rewards if you do.

So how can we step into the space of feeling unharmed ourselves, when currently we may not feel like we are unharmed?

For many, understanding and acting upon Integrity or Wholeness seems far away from human capacity. Yet it is blissful enduring happiness when we do it. It is the nature of Love. It shares in a gentle sweet peace, knowing all is well in that moment.

Why are humans not choosing this?

Question: *Are you yourself not choosing to act from a place of Integrity? If not, for what purpose?*

Action: *Bring to mind a time when you did come from a place of wholeness. For example, you did a good deed for someone less fortunate than you, purely from your heart and space of giving to them, not wishing for or needing anything in return. Recall how that felt to you inside at your heart. I'm sure everyone reading this will* *at some time or other have done something they can recall. This feeling/sensation/knowing you feel as you recall is now your Integrity benchmark. So, when you are observing your behaviours and actions going forward, you will be able to monitor whether or not you are coming from Integrity, by whether or not your 'Integrity Benchmark Feeling' is present or not.*

To enable us to meld more fully with Integrity, it can be helpful to learn how to discipline our mind to think in the language of Love. Not greed, self, me, myself, I, want, deceit, manipulation, shaming, jealousy and so on, but instead by asking: "How can we do this for the benefit of all?" That way we keep ourselves equal and not invalid and keep others also equal and valid. The true nature and Integrity of Love can then flow more freely through us.

We must learn to slow down though in order to first get conscious and be able to observe our behaviours and actions honestly enough, and in turn catch them from, for example, harming others. I know I keep saying it, and my clients will vouch for me(!): "This 24/7 crazy busy bonkers world that has been created by humans is exactly that, crazy busy bonkers and it's too much!" We also distract ourselves enormously. It is our own responsibility though, no-one else's as no-one else is doing this, just we humans. So, take responsibility and choose to change it.

Question: *Are you willing to take responsibility for coming from a place of Integrity, especially outside of those you are closest to, and for some including those you are closest to? Also, include yourself, of course. Often, we are own worst enemy.*

It will take discipline and courage to do this. We can grow courage though in order to leave behind pains from our own childhood, for example, or from yesterday's meeting where you felt bullied, ignored or shamed, last week's fight with your partner and you're still not speaking, last year's fallout with a family member because they did something at Christmas you felt offended by, and so on. We can learn to leave these harms at our feet and then walk forward.

We must take responsibility for our own actions and behaviours though and be consistently asking ourselves, "What harm might this be causing myself and others?" We know in our heart when we are being difficult or unhelpful on purpose to annoy another. We know when are being divisive. We know when we are being dishonest and we or another person will be harmed in the process. We know when we are excluding someone, manipulating them or bullying them. We know when we are being offensive to another. It usually harms us on the inside too and we feel 'hurting' or unsettled deep within. If you are in business, you can always do business so all parties benefit, not just you. If you have an addiction, look deep within and ask yourself: "What part of me is harmed?" This will open the gateway to healing that harm and pain and there is always external help available to support you in this. We know when we are not listening to another and closing our heart to them. Integrity is Whole and true Love contains peace – none of these other actions and behaviours described in this paragraph are or do.

To reiterate, the word 'Integrity' implies 'Wholeness'. It is also linked to the adherence to moral principles, honesty and unity. So when we are coming from a place of Integrity we can remember these qualities: Wholeness, Honesty, Unity, Non-harmfulness. There is no darkness in this and there is nothing unclear about any of that. Integrity underpins Love's essence.

Come into Integrity and let us GIVE this gift to the planet, in gratitude for what she shares with us unconditionally each and every day. We are more often in the state of TAKE from the planet. It is time for us to simply GIVE to her.

Part 2:
This is not Love

The word 'Love' comes from the Old English word 'lufian' which means 'to cherish'. Love does not discriminate. Love treats all equally and although it notices the beauty within each being individually, it also has the capacity to be all encompassing. If we are open to it, the energy of Love is simply there for all of us to meld and flow with, just like the air that we breathe. This way we become Love. To better understand what Love really is, it's perhaps a good idea to take a deeper look at what it is not.

So what is Love not? At this point I will share in summary the unbeneficial and influential experiences of family I've experienced and the 'story' that has played out in my life. I appreciate there will be people reading this who have suffered much worse and others less. Either way, as previously requested, I ask you to suspend judgement of the members of my family as much as you possibly can as you read on – this is important to do for many reasons which, again, I will expand upon later.

As I said in the introduction, I grew up in a created environment that included, but was not limited to, chaos, hate, jealousy, separation, cruelty, anger, dishonesty, secrecy, manipulation, vengefulness, and so on. Yet this was described to me as an environment of Love. This was not Love. I don't doubt many of these elements will touch almost each reader who has experienced at least one of them if not more.

These elements have been 'normalised', but they are not 'Love'.

- Yelling/fighting
- Affairs
- Death and illness
- Abandonment
- Divorce
- Mixed messaging
- Enforced poverty
- Secrecy
- Jealousy, bullying and manipulation

- Inequality
- Alcohol
- Child sexual abuse
- PTSD
- Narcissism
- No empathy
- Lack of closeness
- Selfishness
- Lack of communication
- Little responsibility
- Little remorse and inability to apologise
- Lack of openness and honesty
- Little time, energy and willingness to understand
- Too much future and past, and not enough present
- Chaos and confusion
- Lack of caring guidance

THIS IS NOT LOVE, but it is the family I was born into and existed within while told, THIS IS LOVE.

Part 3: The Impact of Lacking Integrity and Love

This life I was born into was no mistake as far as I'm concerned. It is leading me to unearthing deep Love and sharing in that. So I am not bitter or angry about it anymore. I *have* been, and HUGELY so along the way. I still occasionally feel sad about it because much of the angst has been so unnecessary, but I now know 'this feeling too will pass'.

I grew up in conditions thinking a lot of that stuff was what everyone else experienced and was quite normal. Why wouldn't I think that? It's all I knew.

Let us take a look at each element in some more detail as I understand it and have experienced it – I can only write from that perception for all these elements. I won't go into depths or psychoanalysis because there are plenty of books out there on healing the individual elements. However, I want to give you a flavour of how these impressions on a child can add up for you, the reader, with your own 'story' in mind, but also reading this as a parent or carer. By not being fully conscious and present for children, it can lead to devastating consequences in adulthood, as the bodymind can no longer hold the weight of the darkness and needs to let it go and purify it. I see this often in my complementary therapy practice in the adults I work with. This can be so painful, and what I find tragic each day is that it doesn't have to be this way.

This may not be your understanding or experience, or you may have read something else that explains it better for you. That is all totally as it is, this is just my way of explaining so you can contemplate and come up with your own conclusions.

Some of this is my direct experience, some is what I was told in my family environment or the messaging I received and the way I felt and understood it. The ages I refer to are approximate, but very little was said within my family and much still goes unspoken, so I write from what I can remember and understand.

Again, I ask that you remember to hold Love in your heart as you read on, suspending judgement of the individuals yet paying attention to the behaviours, choices and actions being played out. This may be good practice for when it comes to dealing with people in your own circle.

In summary, this is the impact of what seems to be termed 'normalised love' had on me.

Yelling and fighting

My earliest memory of childhood was my mother and father screaming at each other while my sister and I were put in a room upstairs as they continued to fight and yell downstairs, resulting in my mother retreating for refuge in the bedroom with us. I must have only been 2 or 3 years old, but the imprint of this experience has haunted me and can at times still cause me to freeze, hold my breath and screw my face up, until I get conscious and let it go.

Just for a moment, please pause and contemplate how many more negative experiences may have been layered on top of that until this present day. That was my foundation memory/experience and, as we know, if we build a house and shaky foundations, we are setting it up to have problem after problem later on. Only by knocking it down and starting again with sturdy foundations can there be relief.

Question: *What is your earliest childhood memory? How has this shaped you?*

Question: *What is your child/ren's earliest memory? How has this shaped or is it shaping them?*

Question: *Are you creating sturdy foundations for your child/ren to live from?*

Affairs

Both my mother and father had them. As far as I know, at the time of writing this book, my father remains happily married to Marhi, the lady he left us for back in the early 1970s. My mother's choice of affair in those early years of her marriage to my dad, returned to our lives some years later and was an alcoholic abuser – he passed away several years ago.

My mother was apparently the first to have an affair in my parents' marriage. That's what my dad told me, but because I didn't want to put my mum into more pain or be the cause of anger or arguments between them, I have never asked if that was true. Anyway – regardless who was first – they both seemingly had affairs and our family fractured and separated.

When I was in my late 20s, I remember my dad's wife looking me in the eye and relaying what her father had said to her. He'd said, "If you can look yourself in the eye in a mirror regarding your actions then carry on". I felt sick in the pit of my stomach as she told me this, thinking "how cruel". You look me in the eye and tell me you can totally live with yourself for having encouraged my dad away from me and our young family, and even then, that wasn't enough, you weren't even willing to share him or encourage him to be the father that I needed, and he still might have been. I said nothing in that moment because I'd learned very deeply over the years how to say nothing.

I remember as a teenager thinking, "When it comes to me having a relationship I might as well just be the other woman because the bloke is going to be disloyal to the wife anyway and cause her deep pain. I might as well be the other woman because at least by being her I won't be expecting him to stay and I'll know the pain of him leaving will arrive at some point – so it's a known waiting to happen, whereas being the wife, you don't expect your husband will leave and cause you that much pain, do you." How desperately sad is that? I look back at that young girl now and wish I could parent her, with the knowledge I have now, to navigate such a vulnerable time in her life.

I have subsequently got myself into relationships I shouldn't have. Be sure though, I fully understand I have caused harm and pain – I am responsible for those actions, I regret them, and I am sorry. I have learned the error of my ways. I have also had to walk the path of self-forgiveness regarding this and believe me that is a tough path to tread, but not an impossible one. I hope that gives you hope if you are feeling regretful for any actions you may have taken with regard to affairs.

This demonstrates though the pain and mixed messaging affairs can cause and what they teach children and teenagers. I'm not making judgements on you if you're in this situation, I am though simply asking you to come more into consciousness and honesty about it. Stand in the shoes of any children you may have (no matter their age), which you created in the name of 'Love', and also the partner you are cheating on – give them the gift of grace and dignity.

Also, instead of standing in the shoes of greed and wanting, stand in the shoes of the other. See it from the eyes of the one you are having an affair with. The vulnerability in that other person – because there will be a vulnerability that does not need further abuse. What that being needs is the true nature and Integrity of Love.

Communicate in a space of loving kindness and if you don't know how to, get help, but before it gets that far, wake up. Get conscious about where you are in your partnership and family unit. Being bored or growing apart are not reasons to cause destruction to a young family. Take responsibility. Bring in the true nature and Integrity of Love to your being and those closest to you.

Question: *Are you having an affair – if so, for what purpose?*

Question: *Are you coming from the place in your heart that the true nature and Integrity of Love flows?*

Question: *What words and feelings come to mind?*

Action: *Contemplate these feelings and stand in the shoes of those around you and your actions.*

Action: *Ask yourself, what imprints on others and myself am I creating?*

Action: *Contemplate, is there anyone who you are placing in vulnerability due to your actions? Include yourself too, of course.*

Question: *What are your children not asking, for fear of putting you into pain, and instead holding themselves in confusion?*

Action: *Perhaps in a space of loving kindness you could ask them.*

Action: *If, in your heart you know it to be for the best that you separate from your family unit or relationship – get help to communicate, swallow your pride, be* *gentle with each other, dig deep and enable each other dignity wherever you can. Be honest from your hearts, it will save a lot of pain in the long run, even though it will hurt to begin with. Separate in as much kindness as you can, and in the long term you can then all benefit this way.*

Death and illness

For those who have lost someone dear, it can be shocking, it can rip you to shreds, it can be draining and, mostly, it can take a lot to recover from – some never do.

I was approximately age three when my younger brother Adam died around eight-months-old. I remember when it happened, and the wailing cries from my parents, very clearly. I have been told it was due to silent pneumonia. This must have been so deeply painful for my parents and what they must have carried with them through their lives can only be known by someone who has had such a devastating and engulfing experience. It has rarely been discussed. Despite wanting to know more, apart from a couple of instances, I haven't asked about Adam and I don't know at all how this little soul was beginning to grow and about his essence.

It was done though, in the past, not to be changed and that was it. Going over it and putting my parents further into pain by repeatedly asking about him wouldn't bring him back, so that wasn't an option. The overarching reason for not asking anything was I didn't want to cause my parents further pain. You see that's how deeply and tenderly little children think – they are aligned more closely to the true nature and Integrity of Love and have more ability to allow it to flow through them.

Adam's death probably taught me one of life's greatest lessons naturally though, and I learned it when I was so very young. The lesson being "death is coming to us all and can happen in any moment – death does not discriminate", so I am rarely shocked at death. I can feel sad at the loss, of course, and empathy for others affected and their suffering, but it is the one thing on this earth that cannot be changed, and no matter how much we grieve and suffer painfully, it will not bring that being back to life.

It is therefore far less painful to accept death than not accept it, than playing out the pain and suffering in our lives that goes with that non-acceptance, but this can take deep courage and consciousness.

Of course, if loss has been experienced at the hands of another and laws broken, then energies can be channelled into addressing that, so long as the bodymind understands consciously the lost one will never return – all that fighting for justice will not change what has happened.

In addition to Adam's premature death, my sister was rushed into hospital on numerous occasions – also with pneumonia. She too nearly died. I remember age six being terrified as I stood at the door of the hospital ward watching her lifeless and limp body behind the oxygen tent that she was encased in. I was too terrified to get close in case she also died – she was so poorly. My sister recovered but has suffered a lot with asthma and eczema over the years.

Abandonment

My dad left our family unit when I was about four years old; he decided to abandon us and create a new family, and has not really looked back much since, nor given much in the way of fathership to me along the way. Apparently, my dad's departure was in the same 12-month period my mother's father passed away and my eight-month-old brother – their son – died. This must have been horrific for my mother on so many levels – I have never underestimated that.

Back to the abandonment. I so remember the moment I experienced feeling abandoned, and it wasn't the time my dad told me he was moving to live in Edinburgh when I was eight – although that was another abandonment bombshell at which I cried a lot and told him I didn't want him to leave. Nor was it when he left our family home originally when I was around age four. He was in the navy so away a lot anyway, perhaps that is why. Perhaps it was because my parents shielded me from it. Perhaps it was also because I was very young and so present in the moments with life that I didn't see it as a problem.

Or perhaps the messaging was given in a way that I could handle and accept it. Who knows?

Anyway, it was when I was six, on a Sunday afternoon when my sister and I were taken out by my dad for the afternoon. We were permitted to spend time with him alternate Sundays at that time – oh, and Friday evenings after school because my mother worked late then.

This particular afternoon we had been taken out along with his new girlfriend (I'm not sure if they were yet married) to the Lake District and were happily having a picnic. Dad had bought us an inflatable dinghy for Christmas and it seemed like we were all having a fun day. He played with us in the lake, pulling us around in the dinghy and I remember loving spending time with him – I felt a close bond with my dad and I simply loved being with him and close to him.

Once back on the shoreside I remember being stunned into a black hole of aloneness and almost seeing from a deep black hole deep inside me. I watched as my father frolicked lovingly with his new girlfriend, caressing her as they laughed in joy together. My world as I knew it ended in that moment. I remember thinking my dad doesn't love me anymore, or more so that he loves her much more than me – he's chosen someone else. I have not spoken of this before and as I write I can still see it just as in a movie – that 'disbelief and freeze moment' which my bodymind went into and the numbing moment of being flung into the abyss of lost love and aloneness. Nobody else would have noticed nor even known this happened until now I guess.

A few years later came another abandonment bombshell when my father told me he was moving away to live 200 miles away in Edinburgh with his wife and by now my new little half-brother and they wouldn't be coming back. What is that term, by the way? Half-brother?! If that isn't causing separation in family I don't know what is. I have always insisted he is my brother as is the second one who came along a couple of years later. Both my brothers. Still are, despite us having no contact due to estrangement with my dad.

I remember crying a lot when my dad told me, and I told him I didn't want him to leave. Edinburgh was a five-hour car journey away from my home town in those days – and even further in the head of a vulnerable, not resilient eight-year-old. My dad's wife is Scottish and, of course, what she or they wanted now took priority over my needs. I wasn't heard – what I wanted didn't come into it. I was only a child with no real voice after all, yet my life was about to be hugely affected.

As I evolved, I continued to maintain a fragile 'holiday visits and phone calls' relationship with my father, hanging on and placing myself in front of him even though he didn't really seem interested or to even notice me. I remember having thoughts as that child who oscillated between: "I feel like I'm a nuisance being here and I bet he'll be relieved when I go back to mum's" to "Please do something to show me you do Love me, dad" to "If I place myself in front of you, you have to be confronted with yourself each time you see me and you might just see my pain and talk with me and help me". But that didn't seem to happen in the way I needed it. Meantime, he and my sister didn't speak for the best part of 20 years while my mother and he operated a palpable silent war and still do.

In the last 10 years my father and I have pretty much been estranged. I tried in many ways to have a relationship with my dad, but it has just seemed too difficult for him, so I gave up the fight of putting myself in front of him, not to be seen nor cared about, nor Loved. Now I accept it and don't get sad or try and understand why. I just let it be as he wishes it to be, while doing my best to keep an open heart.

So, the effects of abandonment I've experienced and felt have included: feeling unloved and unlovable, uncared for, uncherished, alone, unprotected, unsupported, unguided, unimportant like a rag doll that can be tossed aside at any point, like I don't have a choice in it, that I can't do anything about it, and voiceless. This has then unconsciously and confusingly played out as patterns in other areas of my life.

Question: *Were you abandoned as a child and can resonate with such feelings? Do you need to release any residing pain being held in your body relating to this? Perhaps you can contemplate this to release it.*

Action: *If you are a mother, father or step-parent of a young child who has or is navigating separation or divorce, please for a time stand in your child's shoes and wonder from their perspective, NOT yours and not from a justification perspective either. Nor from a judgemental perspective, or the view you are 'owner' of the child and you can simply do what you like because you're in charge. Instead, purely from the heart, stand in their shoes. Contemplate how it is to be that child, i.e. to be abandoned. You may wish to gently ask some questions to truly understand how it is to be that vulnerable child.*

Question: *Is it worth breaking that fragile heart or can you work your shit out? I'm sorry for swearing but this burns through so many young children and teenagers and I feel very strongly that with less social media, more guidance and supported communication, as well as more openness to loving kindness there would be fewer damaging break-ups. That's not to say no break-ups, but damaging ones.*

Action: *Contemplate how children may need both their parents equally to grow and develop securely. The first seven years of a child's life are their foundation for the rest of their life – you are responsible for their wellbeing and it is vital you understand this, particularly through these years.*

By the way – if either or any of you are being abused or in danger, I'm not including you. Do what you need to keep yourselves safe.

Divorce

My parents split up and divorced in the early 1970s, before I even started school. Back then divorce was still fairly unusual, and I felt the shame and lowering of being from a divorced family. I was one of only a few in my school year at that time. I grew up feeling less than those around me, like I was different and not quite acceptable, lowly in a way, almost dirty. If I went to school friends' houses, I often had a feeling they were thinking "she's the one from the divorced family". I grew up feeling not worthy of staying for. On the flip side, I then felt overly grateful if someone was accepting of me or actually took an interest in me and mostly if someone truly shared 'time' with me.

My father was a submariner and the lady he chose to leave us for and create a new family with, Marhi, was a nurse. Once I became aware of this new woman my dad was to marry, I simply got on with it. I quite liked the way she spent time with me, teaching me to tell the time, knitting and baking with me – we'd make my dad an orange cake as a surprise on Sunday afternoons while he was doing jobs like decorating and creating a vegetable patch in the garden. I suspect he knew he'd be getting a cake, but he joyfully went along with my excitement to surprise him each time.

So, this is where I believe young children can be resilient, but it's a fine line and mostly children are not resilient. If they were, so many of those children wouldn't feel the need to seek therapy once into adulthood, would they?

In the very early years I adapted to the change because I was young and had no baggage attached to it myself and neither was there a choice. I just knew I went to dad's on Friday evenings and every other Sunday. However, what I wasn't resilient about was my dad moving away and creating another family, not seeing him regularly and not being held by him. As a vulnerable child caught in the midst of contentious and warring parents, I missed out on the cherishing and nourishment I needed. As time went on and I got older I became aware of the desperate circumstances my dad left us in, according to my mother, sister and family friends. This was their noise. As far as I know my father is still happily married to Marhi who he left us for and I have never had a problem with that aspect – they have clearly been right for each other. Had he gone off 'tag lag' from one relationship to another, I may have felt differently. What I have struggled with though is not having a present father. Not having his care, protection, guidance or support, nor one who has been interested in my growth, life, joys and struggles.

Often, I have felt bereft of all of this and have suffered deeply because of it. I sometimes watch the TV programme *Long Lost Family* with Davina McCall and Nicky Campbell as they reunite families who have gone through adoptions and lost contact for years. I bawl my eyes out at the pain and wasted years these individuals endure through forced separation, and it is so heart-warming when they are reunited – you can almost see the pain and weight lift physically from them. Then the question arises in me: how can a father knowingly still choose to abandon his creation and not be interested in his own flesh and blood and want to share together in life and Love? But he doesn't want to have anything to do with me or he hasn't got the capability; either way he will have his reasons for that.

I remember my dad saying years ago: "Carmen, put in a room and asked to comment on what has gone on over the years, your mother, your sister, you and I will all have different opinions on what happened, and we will all see it differently." I didn't doubt he was right.

During those early years of the divorce, I obviously had little knowledge of what was going on behind the scenes regarding my parents' separation – and still don't know really … well, apart from hearing it was beyond contentious.

What I do know is that as a child I felt split in two and a feeling of uncertainty of how I should be at my dad's new house. I remember asking my dad's permission and out of politeness, "Dad, please may I go to the toilet?" I remember him scooping me up saying, "You're in your home, you don't have to ask." But I didn't feel like I was in my home – it was strange, and I felt like a visitor. Also, I remember a nervousness of saying something that might upset my mum and cause her pain if I mentioned my dad and his new wife, and the fear of furious anger if I mentioned mum to my dad and his wife. Tension was palpable at every move.

So, I learned to close down to my naturalness and try and instead to be pleasing to those around me.

I'd lost my authenticity – I had to perform a version of Carmen and I was eight years old.

How is this teaching a child to grow out of childhood into independence in their true essence and in the true nature and Integrity of Love? It just so isn't. It's desperately sad for all concerned. So much unnecessary suffering.

I therefore implore you to look deep into your hearts and that of your young child/ren before getting anywhere near close to separation or divorce. Communicate, get help, do whatever you can and if you still can't work it out – then at least drop the negativities of your ego and judgementalness. Separate in as much kindness as possible, for the sake of all parties and continually ask yourself at each step of the way: "What would the true nature and Integrity of Love do?"

Delete the general phrase: "Children are resilient, they'll be ok". IT'S NOT TRUE! If children are so resilient, then why are so many children and adults in therapy these days, dealing with and healing from childhood experiences? Additionally, why are statistics in 2018 showing one quarter of all girls have self-harmed by the age of 14, and so on…?

Question: *Are you performing an inauthentic version of you?*

Question: *How authentic are your actions and the words you speak?*

Question: *Are you nurturing your child/ren to be in their authenticity?*

Mixed messaging

When there is a lot of chaos around, ill feeling, busy-ness and survival going on, sadly so many mixed messages can arise.

I remember when I was around six years old, my sister was ill in hospital with pneumonia and I was sent to friends to be taken care of. I couldn't understand why I didn't go to my dad's as there were two people there who could look after me. There will no doubt have been reasons that involved work, as well as anger and arguments.

Anyway – once my sister was out of hospital and on the road to recovery, my dad gave me a present just for me because I'd been so well behaved during the period my sister had been ill. With his Irish lilt, he said I'd been "not a bother". He'd fixed an old radio. I can still feel the joy of receiving something just for me with all that intentional kindness behind it. That is such a wonderful imprint. I took it home to show my mum, and distinctly remember her telling me "I'm sorry I can't afford to give you anything like that – but I'll give you my love". In that moment, I heard "Your dad has given to you but not his love. He can afford to give you things as he has more money than we do, but I love you." I probably got the messaging wrong, but the imprint on that young child was a negative one. Couldn't my mother have just allowed me to be joyful and listen to my radio with Love flowing through my heart each time because my dad had made me this special gift? Each time I played it, part of that joy was missing because I felt guilty for having the radio. Her feelings were more important than mine in that moment and I had to be secret at any small amount of joy I had in listening to my new radio. It was tinged with sadness – I wasn't allowed full joy.

On another occasion I remember being upset and asking my mother: "Why did my brother Adam have to die?" and, among other reasons, the reply included: "I couldn't have afforded to feed three children with dad gone and everything so perhaps that's why he was taken away." Again, this may not have been exactly how she said or intended it, but that is the messaging I took into my heart and I distinctly remember immediately feeling guilty for being alive, wishing I could have changed places with Adam, so he could have had life. I was about eight at the time.

Then in my early 20s, my dad's wife once remarked: "When you were little, your mother shopped for your food at M&S; we've never done that, we were saving every penny we had." It seemed a petty thing to say. And was she hoping I'd pass that message back to my mother? I never did pass messages between the 'sides'.

She was right though – my mother did shop for some of our food at M&S. So how did this fit with us being poor? I couldn't work it out, and, again, I didn't dare ask the question for fear of causing more pain between my parents as they continued their war in silence. The mere mention of my mother to my father was often met with silence or a groan followed by the words "That woman!", while my mother met me with bitter silence if I mentioned him. Each time I would be flung back into tension and those feelings of split loyalties and confusion. This is nowhere near the realm of the true nature and Integrity of Love. Yet, interestingly, both are not bad people, both are just trying to get through life in the way that is right for them and how they know best, with the internal and external resources they have available to them as human beings. My parents have been good to me in other ways – it hasn't all been bad, but it hasn't been a balance for sure.

Still though, neither seem to have learned about the true nature and Integrity of Love. I feel sad, because why would anyone not want to know what it feels like to exist in such gentle and powerful bliss, but instead choose to reside where they are?

Question: *Are you aware of how many mixed messages you are putting out into the world?*

Question: *Do you communicate to ensure people understand where you are coming from clearly?*

Question: *Are you playing people off against each other? If so, why, and how is this kind? How does it help raise the level of Integrity for humanity and the planet?*

Action: *If you are in the middle of separation or divorce, or a family feud, or a work negotiation, contemplate how you can communicate clearly and in honesty so nobody misunderstands you, but especially young children whom you say you Love.*

Obviously, people will always interpret things as they hear them, but as individuals we have a responsibility to ensure we are communicating clearly.

Enforced poverty

Following the divorce, apparently my father held back on making sufficient maintenance payments and my mother had to take him to court to get it adjusted, while at the same time she worked very hard to earn enough to provide for us, juggling bringing up two young children, one of whom was often poorly. This all was not long after she'd lost her father, and they had lost their son. Times were also very different in the 1970s. Choosing not to provide for your family is not Love though and I wonder how this sits with my father's conscience.

As you can begin to ascertain, poverty seemed to swamp my little mind as a child and I took that into adulthood with me, with external and internal messaging.

"Poor Carmen, she's from the divorced family."

"Poor Carmen, her dad abandoned her."

"Poor Carmen, she can't afford it."

"Her poor mum and those children – it's all so sad."

"What's wrong we me that I am not worth staying for? Clearly I am not enough."

"Poor Carmen, she doesn't have a lot of luck."

"I won't ask for it/help because I know we are poor"

"I can't say how I want it to be – my voice doesn't mean anything."

"I can't afford it."

"I can't have."

…and so on…

When my father departed, my mother moved us into a flat above a dental surgery. Apparently, the kind-hearted dentist enabled us to live there rent free until my mother could buy a house and move us elsewhere. I did not hear about this until adulthood of course, and too late to thank this dentist from the bottom of my heart for his generous heart, because by then he had passed away. But what a kind soul. Who does that sort of thing these days? The dentist would never receive anything from me, not even a thank you, yet he chose to allow us to live in a flat he owned because he was clearly not a greedy man. Despite the fact that he could have earned rent from it during that time, he simply allowed the true nature and Integrity of Love to flow through him.

After that my mum, sister and I then moved into a two-up-two-down terraced house, which had a sink balanced on two columns of bricks when my mother bought it. At that time grants were being made available from the local council to help those in need make houses habitable. My mother applied and was successful.

She did not take money from the state in the form of benefits for us at any time. Instead she worked part time as a hairdresser and slowly slowly created her own business owning a hairdressing salon. She always worked hard, she also socialised a fair bit and it felt like there was little true time of her being present for me in her life. I understand it in the early years, she was utterly doing her best, but when I became an adult and when she has had more financial security, I do not. I guess it is her habit and the imprints that formed within her though. Habits are hard for we humans to break and it can be so difficult without the willingness and determination to make changes.

Anyway, back to the terraced house – the outside loo was freezing to go to in the mornings and not much fun on winter evenings either. I shared a bedroom with my sister, who was often physically poorly. As I mentioned earlier, she suffered pneumonia twice and nearly died, and she also suffered from severe asthma and eczema. The flooring in our bedroom had to be lino as that was deemed healthier for my sister. I also remember the paraffin oil lamp burning shortly before we went to bed as there was no other form of heating upstairs. We had a coal fire in the front room, and my job was to lay the fire ready to be lit, so when my mum came home from work she could light it and warmth could begin to glow. Electricity came on as long as 10p and 50p pieces had been put in the meter; sometimes there were no 50p coins.

As I said, along with the grant, my mother worked hard and slowly over the years and she was able make more improvements to create a home. The kitchen was first: that got a gas fire and an extension to house a bathroom. The route out of the kitchen finally led to an indoor toilet and proper basin and bath, instead of the kitchen sink our mother would wash us in before then. After that came central heating – it was bliss! Small mercies, hey….?

As I mentioned, my sister suffered horrendously with eczema and to this day I can still feel the pain in the screams that came from that bathroom as my mum had to put her in the bath, so the weeping scabs on her legs would hurt just that bit less as she peeled my sister's socks off. The pain my sister had to endure physically must have been horrendous for those screams to be as agonising and piercing as they were. Bearing witness to the pain my mum and sister were experiencing was heartbreaking and traumatic. Even now my heart breaks and the tears roll down my face as I write this, feeling their pain.

Question: *Are you placing anyone in poverty, not just financially, but in their worthiness as a human being?*

Question: *Why are you choosing to do this and can you change it?*

Question: *Are you placing yourself into poverty consciousness?*

Action: *Help yourself come to understand that we are all equal. Do this with the help of someone who can assist you.*

Action: *If you are fortunate and have the financial resources, do something like the kind dentist did. If you aren't so fortunate financially, learn from someone who is, or accept it in your heart and be okay with it. Perhaps it is not your time in this life time to be financially well off and you have other things to learn.*

Secrecy

This for me is one of the cruellest and deepest forms of manipulation I feel I have experienced. A lot of things unsaid instead of honesty and openness; the darkness of whispering and much swept under the carpet. The word 'secret' has its roots in the meaning 'to separate' and this is exactly what it does.

In my mother's infinite wisdom (not) for example, she would never tell my sister and I off in front of each other, thus missing an opportunity to teach us and guide us in openness. My sister was vile to me, locking me in the house so I couldn't go and play out with my friends when they called for me. She couldn't let us be equal, let alone think of me as more capable at some things than she was. She always needed to be more, the best, to be first, to 'win'. Yet half the time I wasn't playing her game and instead I let her battle against herself, but she was so caught up in the 'win' she didn't even realise the reality of what was going on. She would also find it very difficult to share anything with me and when I complained about any of it, my mother seemed to do nothing. This is a theme by the way – her doing very little in the form of mothering guidance. Years later she told me she used to speak to my sister separately about her treatment of me, in other words in secret. However, she didn't have the notion to tell me that's what she'd done, so again I grew up misinformed thinking my sister always got away with blue murder. Why couldn't she just have sat us round the table and talked with us and taught us how to discuss things, how to be forgiving, how to respect each other, how to bring in Love? She couldn't because she hadn't been taught how to by her own parents, from what I've gleaned along the way.

What we did as children in my mother's home was not encouraged or even allowed to be spoken of at my father's home with his new wife, and therefore the split of loyalties was sown, and duality created, as I thought it then only fair not to talk of experiences at my father's home to my mother. I found it difficult being loyal to both – it felt like being inside a dark box and keeping a lid on it all. Occasionally I would let things slip out. Sometimes because the dark box was full to the brim, and sometimes by accident. Someone would then feel pain though and all because of my lack of control of the dark box. I learned to internalise almost everything from that tender age, i.e. around six, and instead presented a happy demeanour. When I look back on photos from my childhood, there isn't peace in my face, but a shyness and a nervousness, uncertainty and deep sorrowfulness – it's plain to see, so why did no adult pick up on that and help me in a way that I understood was help?

There were other incidents such as when visiting my father during the divorce years and being scolded by my sister: "Mum said we're not allowed to talk about that in front of them." I haven't a clue what this was about, but my dad's wife relayed this story numerous times in my adult life saying how shocked they were to hear my sister scolding me. She couldn't tell me what I'd said, so I just thought "Nasty bitch, if you can't tell me the whole story then why tell me at all now? I'm not doing your dirty work for you and relaying that message back to my mother!" I've also often thought how sad for two little children to be living in such friction and fear, because adults can't seem to Love and instead need one-upmanship and to play games because they are in pain and that is more overwhelmingly paramount than the wellbeing of their young and vulnerable children. There was simply no thought to stand in the shoes of their tiny children and be present in that. Or even just stand holding the space in the moments of utter confusion and be present with us explaining that we were safe, that we could be who we naturally are and bring in the true nature and Integrity of Love. They didn't because they hadn't been taught how either I guess. They didn't because they were caught up in the fight too.

Know though, as people and especially as parents our words are more powerful than we realise in each moment, and may I encourage you to choose them consciously and wisely always. Toltec, Don Miguel Ruiz, writes in his book *The Four Agreements* about "Being Impeccable with Your Word". I invite you to read it. Our words are so powerful and as he explains, "they can change or destroy lives in a moment".

This will mean being awake in each moment. This is the promise you really make when you consciously bring a child/ren into this world. If you don't have the capability to do this, get help, it is out there. Or simply hold in your continuous consciousness: "What would the true nature and Integrity of Love do right now?"

Secrecy, albeit in a different form, continued and I endured living in fear every day of being sexually abused by my mother's alcoholic boyfriend for five of my childhood and teenage years. More of this later though.

I used to say my epitaph will read "What Goes Unsaid Causes the Problems". What I mean by this is in order to flush through the nonsense and drama of painful emotions, misunderstandings and mental torture, courage is required to sit round a table and discuss things through to resolution, held in a space of the true nature and Integrity of Love, kindness and the intention of healing. Often hearing and feeling painfulness, but safe in the knowledge that peace will arise at the end of the discussion, is more powerful than we realise.

Question: *How often do you create the opportunity in your family to sit together and discuss where you are as a family, what family means to you, indeed encouraging each family member to acknowledge the other and ironing out any frictions so you can move forward into more peace, however that may be?*

Action: *Create opportunities for this to arise and do it within a space where you are holding the energy of loving kindness with you.*

Jealousy, bullying and manipulation

Along my path when I've been healing my soul and light, the concept of "choosing the family you are born into" has arisen.

For anyone not familiar with this concept, this is when, as a spirit, before we come into this human life, we choose our parents and which family to enter so we can heal and purify the stuff we need to in this lifetime. This may sound a bit whacky to some, but it has to do with archetypes and soul groups. Caroline Myss is a great resource on this stuff if you are interested to know more.

Anyway, what I was going to say is if this concept is true, I chose big style! I read a book years ago by Wayne Dwyer called *There is a Spiritual Solution to Every Problem* (wonderful read) where he said words similar to: "The people who press our buttons the most are often our best teachers". My sister was certainly in that camp for me.

In the family unit, I often felt as though I ruined my sister's life by being born and nobody was telling me any different. However, I have for most of my life, subtly and sometimes not so subtly, tried to help my sister come to know what the true nature and Integrity of Love is and yet I haven't been able to. As Margaret Thatcher once said, "This lady is not for turning" and my sister certainly hasn't been. I say that smiling, by the way. However, this is now also another thing I accept these days and I do not need to try and change it.

My sister and I are very different in most aspects including personality and character. I think the only things we have in common are our parents, our pain, the need for healing from our childhood, and the fact we breathe. She has often shown insufferable cruelty, jealousy, bullying and controlling behaviour towards me, while also wreaking havoc within our family. Jealousy is a form of pain.

One situation shocked me to my core though when she openly and with no awareness demonstrated her raw and cruel thought process. At my nephew's christening, we were standing together in the church when one of my sister's friends from the congregation came over to speak to us and, in due course, my sister introduced me. The chap asked if I was going to be godmother, to which I replied "No, I'm not" with a smile. It was a genuine smile. I totally understood that my sister wanted members of the faith she followed to be godparents to her son and I didn't have a problem with it at all, that was her right and choice after all. However, what I didn't expect was my sister's follow-on comment when she said, "We've gone for quality, not quantity" as she pointed to the Minister on the other side of the church. He and his wife were due to be godparents, along with a family friend who works within the church and was dialled into the service from the UK.

I let a lot go over the years where my sister's behaviour is concerned, but when I have reached my limit and had enough of not reacting to her appalling behaviour towards me and others, I have on numerous occasions let her know about it and it shocks her into utter disbelief that she could possibly be the one behaving imperfectly. Until the last couple of years, she really has had no idea the impact her jealous, cruel and bullying behaviour has had on me throughout our lives. Ultimately though I try to understand and realise that my sister is suffering. Suffering, because our childhood was tough and damaging. Suffering, because she can never be wrong. Suffering, because her heart is so closed. We are both sensitive beings and the imprints we took on went deep for each of us in different ways. We have both sought healing support outside of family/friends for our pain in different ways: she through Christian Faith; I through Spirituality and Dharma teachings. I cannot be sure I speak for my sister, of course, but my sense is that both of us, like many others, would just like to reside in lasting peace, happiness and Love.

I no longer tolerate my sister's recklessness though where I am concerned. I gave her plenty of opportunities over a seven-year period to resolve our differences, but especially the last two years, when I tried to bring our family into unity with the intention of creating peace between all of us and for all of us. Perhaps you, like I, question why I was doing this and not my mother? Good question.

My sister did not take up these opportunities though; instead she still seemed to want revenge, while maintaining a steadfast unwillingness to forgive and move on in those relationships. At one point we met up, and she blatantly lied to get me there. I had said, "If you're willing to come to the table in peace then I'm happy to meet." She wrote back agreeing to that. We met on neutral territory and once we were together it quickly became apparent that she had in fact come to the table with a prepared dialogue full of revenge which she unwaveringly delivered. When I pointed out that she didn't seem to have come to the table in peace, she replied, "I haven't; you wouldn't have come otherwise." In hindsight, I should have perhaps quietly left at that point, but I didn't. I chose to stay and take the hit, via the next layer of vicious verbal onslaught, including being told I was "vacuous" because I wanted peace to be given a chance to reside within our family. I listened and then told her she was my sister and I 'Loved' her and that drawing a line in the sand was necessary. I sincerely meant it because I had peace in my heart and was working very hard to encourage our family into peace. She was not for letting go though.

So, I now just get on with my life and hold the wish that she too finds peace in her heart at some point. I have learned to Love myself and acknowledge my humanness in the process too. I do not need to be repeatedly on the receiving end of cruel, bullying and malicious behaviour – I can simply move myself away from it and keep an open heart.

Question: *Have you ever bullied anyone? You know in your heart if you have, even if it is a mild attempt and may include manipulation.*

Question: *For what purpose do you choose to cause someone else and yourself pain in this way?*

Question: *Are you being manipulated or bullied? Do you need support in order for this to end?*

Question: *What can you do to find peace in your heart, so the bully or jealous being cannot affect you?*

I remember bullying at school: a group of girls, including me, used to name call a particular girl each time she passed us between lessons at school, and I often led the name calling. I can still see the look of dread in her eyes as she steeled herself to walk past us. In later life, I have often wondered about her and the cruel imprints I must have left her with. Energetically I have apologised, and I hope she has felt my remorse and has been able to accept my apology. I am so sorry to her that I ever did that, and I deeply hope she recovered from all the bullying – sadly I know other children bullied her too.

I also remember stopping three boys bullying another boy when I was a school Prefect. The injustice that one boy was suffering as he was taunted and hit, was deeply painful to witness, yet no one else around seemed to notice or care. So, I went over to them and scolded them in true Prefect style as you could back then. They ran off. I casually checked the lone figure was okay as he pulled his jacket back on; being a girl, I didn't want to embarrass him and cause the potential for further bullying, but I could see he was relieved and okay.

Question: *Are you jealous of someone? Are you blocking them in any way?*

Action: *Contemplate that if you had what that person you are jealous of has, would you still be jealous of them?*

Question: *Do you really 'need' or 'want' what that other person has?*

Question: *Will it impact on anyone by chasing it down and is the true nature and Integrity of Love present when jealousy is present?*

Action: *When jealousy arises, contemplate: "For what purpose am I jealous?" Then ask the true nature and Integrity of Love to flow through you to dispel your jealousy and help you to then move forward without incorporating the emotion of jealousy. Ask: "What would the true nature and Integrity of Love do right now?" and then do it!*

Action: *Learn to give selflessly to the person you are jealous of instead of taking from them. This takes a lot of courage and determination to conquer the ego within, because it is the ego running this behaviour.*

Inequality

My dad and his wife chose to send my brothers to a prestigious private school while we lived a restricted life financially and at most turns were told, "No, we can't afford it". We certainly didn't go to private school like my brothers either. There is a slight irony here in that the school they went to offers free places to fatherless children. I also remember around the age of six I said to my dad's wife "I want xyz" and she replied, "I want never gets." She was no doubt teaching me manners, but it also felt like there was more to it as well. Again, as I was sensitive, it went deep and I've had to unlearn it, but to this day I find it really hard and instead often run the pattern of "I can't have, but others can".

Question: *Do you treat your children and step-children unequally? If so, why do you choose to do this?*

Question: *Are all children or indeed all beings not deserving of equal regard and Love?*

Action: *Observe how and where you treat beings unequally and perhaps begin to address this. Love does not discriminate, Love regards all equally and although it notices the beauty within each being individually it still does not discriminate – it is all encompassing.*

Action: *Contemplate how you may look at flowers in a vase or trees in the countryside. One is no less deserving of acceptance than the other, is it? Yet we often do this regarding sentient beings, don't we?*

Action: *Come into Wholeness, Honesty, Unity, Non-harmfulness as much as possible with all beings and allow the true nature and Integrity of Love to flow through and round you, and thus to them.*

Alcohol

Alcohol helps very few people. My mother's partner was an alcoholic and we suffered hugely because of this, the worst aspect being sexually abused as children.

I remember on occasions as a teenager when doing the housework for my mother at the weekend I'd find empty bottles of vodka stashed behind the sofa cushions where he'd been sitting watching the TV the night before. When I showed my mother, she just hushed it away and told me to carry on with the cleaning.

One night he was followed home by the police. Unaware of his actions, he'd fallen asleep at the wheel of his car when pulled up at a set of traffic lights 15 miles from our home. A lady had seen it from her front room and called the police and they picked him up. Again, it was all swept under the carpet and not discussed openly in the family or even when I asked questions – I was just hushed and silenced, yet again.

After the abuse came to light, my mother suggested I try going to meetings at Alateen – part of Al-Anon but the supporting arm for teenagers affected by alcoholics. She said we needed to help him and they would be able to help me do that and understand him. WTF! HELP HIM?! WHAT ABOUT MEEEEEEEEE?! What help did she give me and how did she try and understand me? I didn't go to

Alateen. Perhaps if she'd introduced it to me more as a way to help me to come to terms with what I'd been through at the hands of an alcoholic, I might have been more inclined, but at age 15 in the depths of trauma I just wanted to run as far away as I could now that I was free.

There are some people I know who just smile under the influence of alcohol, but for the vast majority it is poison and causes people to create damage on an epic scale. Consumed in excess, this fluid helps no-one. It alters the being. It numbs pain. It changes the mind. It is addictive. It neither feeds nor nourishes the bodymind positively in any way, shape or form. Under excess influence, people behave recklessly. It simply has nothing to do with nor contributes towards the true nature and Integrity of Love and its flow.

Although I have no experience of recreational drugs in my family, and I may be wrong here so forgive me if I am, but I imagine similar recklessness that derives from the consumption of alcohol can be applied to drugs. You can also replace or add the word drugs where alcohol exists in this text if it feels appropriate for you.

I'm not saying alcohol should be banned for everyone, of course, but we need to ask ourselves consciously in the moment before drinking it – how will drinking this equally benefit me and those around me with the actions I may take under its influence?

In the past I have behaved utterly recklessly under the influence of alcohol. It gave me a let-out to not give a shit when I was in my 20s, or that's how I went into a night of social drinking with friends. It numbs pain, as many of us know.

Interestingly, in my late 20s, I did an experiment and committed to not drinking alcohol for a year. I did it because the thought went through my mind; "If I carry on drinking like this – getting smashed on nights out with friends in the name of fun – I will end up in the gutter."

I didn't drink during the week at all but on the weekends, I binged and drank purely to get smashed under the guise of a 'good fun night out'. I became fed up of waking after 'the night before' feeling rubbish and thinking "I can't fully remember what I said, but I know I will have said something awful (which wouldn't enter my sober mind) and who do I need to apologise to?"

Accompanying that were feelings of self-loathing, which also took me even further away from being able to accept and have Love for myself and I was actually abandoning my true nature, the truly authentic being I am more able to bring forth these days. The true nature and Integrity of Love certainly wasn't able to shine brightly through the cloud storm that was me back then.

Although I didn't realise it at the time, this experiment was actually the beginning of my journey back to authentic light. I didn't find it difficult because I don't have alcoholic tendencies, despite others in my family having drink problems. Therefore, I don't buy it that alcoholism is genetic. This, of course, is just my personal view. Instead I believe an alcoholic is a suffering unconscious human being trying to numb their pain and it goes too far, or it is a formed habit that gets out of control, but at core, it is still likely to include dissatisfaction of self and deep feelings of, for example, unworthiness, frustration, anger, sadness, fear and guilt.

What I actually found more difficult during this experimental year was people's judgementalness. The number of times I heard my so-called friends saying "how boring" when I asked for an orange juice or sparkling water instead of usual copious amounts of poison I had previously put into my body. It struck me during that time how difficult it must be for someone simply trying to cut down their intake of alcohol, let alone an alcoholic steeling themselves to say "no" in such a situation. I didn't have to really apply any force to not having an alcoholic drink as it was my wish and I was choosing to do it. I didn't experience the difficulty of not being able to resist, but for someone who finds it hard to resist alcohol, I could see how as fellow humans we don't make it easy for them.

Action: *Perhaps, consider this next time you're at a party and thinking or even saying "how boring" someone is for not drinking, and all the feelings and emotions that might race around inside that person, just because you perhaps feel uncomfortable that they are choosing not to drink alcohol.*

Question: *For what purpose do I drink alcohol?*

Question: *Is my state under the influence of alcohol the true nature and Integrity of Love?*

Question: *Do I drink so I am different from my natural state and essence? In other words, what am I dissatisfied with?*

Question: *Do I encourage others to drink because I feel uncomfortable that they aren't?*

Question: *Does drinking alcohol numb any pain within me?*

Action: *Reduce your intake if in your heart you know others don't benefit and neither do you.*

Action: *If your intake has gone up without you really noticing, understand you are not living consciously and begin the process of doing so – you will see life in a much more vibrant and clear way and in a way that brings joy and peace to the fore.*

Action: *If you drink to numb your pain, seek help from one who has the capability to help you. Don't feel embarrassed or ashamed, you will be exercising courageousness.*

Action: *If you drink in excess for whatever reason, take action to reduce or stop it. You will feel better mentally, emotionally and spiritually. There will be pain along the way, but you will be healing that pain and clearing your being. You CAN do this.*

Action: *Seek help if it has got hold of you, so that you can heal, and the true nature and Integrity of Love can fully flow through you – it is a much more beautiful, kind and inspiring thing to flow through you than alcohol – I assure you of this. You can make the change – grow the wish to choose to change it.*

Action: *Learn to Love and accept yourself fully in your natural state and essence.*

Child sexual abuse

The first time it happened I was 10 years old. My sister and I were standing at the piano performing for our mother – my sister was playing the piano and I was playing the flute. My mother's new boyfriend knelt down between us facing the piano and put his arms round us. His hand reached too far round my tiny little body and then I was touched inappropriately. I froze on the inside and tried to edge myself away, while having to continue to perform musically and in person. As I've explained, the performance always had to go on – that's what we did in our family – we performed even under extreme stress and torture so as not to let anyone think we were anything but alright and happy. So the performance went on.

My mother was standing behind all of us and I doubt she would have noticed. Somehow I knew he shouldn't have done that, but in the confusion and with the innocence of a child's mind, I thought he perhaps didn't mean to and it was a mistake.

Turns out he was a paedophile, so clearly it wasn't a mistake. The abuse was subtle, sneaky, intermittent, and terrifying over a five-year period.

Despite my mother knowing of the abuse for a number of those latter years, we all still stayed living under the same roof without it being discussed or addressed openly. The secrecy surrounding this was only unearthed because on the evening of Live Aid in 1985 I had been home alone with my mother's partner and ended up having to lock myself in the bathroom until my mother and sister came home so I could keep myself safe from what I thought would be nothing less than rape. My sister arrived home first and I ran to her screaming in terror, then when our mother arrived I told her what had happened. On that same evening I heard my sister had been experiencing similar abuse and to protect herself had been sleeping with a hammer under her pillow – just in case she was attacked. I had no clue about my sister's terror and neither did she about mine. We were then taken to stay with one of my mum's friends. I was encouraged to speak to her daughter, who clearly had her own terror from having to live in an alcoholic-infused family environment. I remember thinking that night, "THIS IS ALL SO SHITTILY WRONG, WHY SHOULD WE TEENAGERS BE SUBJECTED TO THIS BECAUSE OF STUPID AND SELFISH ADULTS?" I was so angry and I was hurting. We then roamed for over a week staying with other family friends. I got more and more angry, wondering why we were the ones roaming. Why did he get to stay in the house? However, my mother then took us back to live in that hell hole while the perpetrator was still there, until things could be arranged. I was terrified again but this time it was accompanied by anger which burned furiously inside me. I was like a volcano about to explode but couldn't as I'd been taught not to, but nor was I taught how to handle the anger burning inside.

Add to this further and I was told I wasn't allowed to talk to anyone about the abuse. At the time I didn't question that, because 'secrecy' was something our family did on an epic scale after all – it was 'normalised'.

I later learned this was because my mother was afraid the abuser might lose his job and she might be financially burdened again. WTF – IT WAS ALL ABOUT HER AGAIN! She also told me she was fearful we would be taken into care and that would be worse. WORSE FOR WHO? It couldn't get any worse in my view and, in fact, at that time I thought a foster family might be more loving and caring than where I had been living.

A while later I remember telling my best friend. I swore her to secrecy too but then lived in fear of others finding out once I'd done that. It was hell. All I wanted to do was scream it from the roof tops and tell everyone about this hell so that justice would be done and the abuser would get his comeuppance. I wanted to tell my uncle, so he would break the perpetrator's legs. I wanted so much harm to come to him! Of course this never happened – the secret just went deeper as I continued to behave and do as I was told.

To this day, I still don't understand the madness and cruelty of it all, but the difference is nor do I try to anymore. Instead, I fully accept it happened and it's in the past. It took a lot of courage, therapy and inner work to come to this point of peace. It was wrong, totally wrong that it happened, but I can say in Integrity, I accept it happened and I no longer fight myself inside to try and make it any different than it was.

As I've said before, I have a challenging mind where my mother's behaviour and actions are concerned. I have Love for my mother, I always have and always will, but this scarred our relationship, and even more so because it wasn't allowed to be discussed so healing could not begin between us or our family as a unit. I have myself forgiven her for it though, and I also choose to keep my distance now for various reasons, not just this, but it includes me sharing in Love for myself and keeping myself equal.

Meantime, in more recent years I've watched on TV how it has come to light, bodies responsible for children's welfare in the community, such as football clubs, care homes, specific industries, universities and so on, have been riddled with abuse. This is so painful to watch for most people. These survivors who have been speaking out have demonstrated such courage. The brokenness of these people as they have steeled themselves to this point of disclosing so publicly is painfully evident. They are worthy of great empathy and support through their healing journey.

Also worthy of great empathy and support are all those anonymous people who have remained quiet about the sexual abuse they suffered as children within their own families and homes. They along with anyone who has suffered such abuse will have seen those same images on TV and it will have undoubtedly caused their pain to rear to the surface of their lives, just as it did yet again for me when I watched those images. For me, this is shortly followed by the gathering of inner strength to turn inwards to be in peace and then move forward in life. However, I am fortunate that I have chosen to heal my pain, many have not been able to do this and for them my heart floods with deep compassion and hope that one day they will recover.

It should be remembered that sexual abuse is rife in normal everyday homes. At the time of writing this, NSPCC statistics show that 1 in 20 children have been sexually abused – that's on average one to two children in a child's school class. One in every three children does not report the abuse.

The choices and actions behind these figures are deplorable and I feel justified in that judgement.

That said, all these men and women who have committed these deplorable acts have been raised by parents. They are regular beings who go home to their families and commit heinous crimes. So parents, I have a simple question for you:

What are you doing to teach your children that sexual abuse is utterly deplorable and wrong? It is not the true nature and Integrity of Love.

Action: *Have courage, discuss it in your family.*

Action: *Ensure your child/ren are taught how to treat others with the true nature and Integrity of Love flowing in mind, especially as they evolve through adolescence.*

Action: *Raise your boys and girls in the art of dignity and compassion holding all beings in kindness, including themselves.*

Child sex abuse is ingrained in our society like a cancer and needs to be rooted out at its core for the sake of future generations and their peace. It is going to be a challenge for us to do this but do this we must. So, for example, if there is petty jibing among peers, stamp it out loud and clear – we must catch this at the foundation level for the sake of future generations.

From the brief bit I've seen of Steve Biddulph's work – author of *Raising Boys* – he talks eloquently of educating boys about not watching porn. Parents, you have a duty to do this. It is your responsibility. Take appropriate action.

Question: *Have you or do you talk to your son(s) about the damaging effects of porn, or do you choose not to because it's either embarrassing or actually you like to look at it yourself?*

Question: *Are you teaching your sons appropriate boundaries where girls are concerned? Are you teaching them how to control themselves?*

Question: *Have you spoken to your daughter(s) about what is acceptable and not acceptable where sexual matters are concerned? This is not for the schools and governments to do or fund. It is your job as a responsible parent to have these conversations.*

My mother left books around for my sister and I to read by ourselves in order to teach us how our body would change through adolescence, and at school we were given a one-hour talk about what sex is and what a condom is. That was the extent of teaching I was provided about sexual matters and that is abominable.

Action: *Ditch any embarrassment and the destructiveness of your ego! Communicate openly with your child/ren. I can assure you, your embarrassment is nothing compared with the hell of recovering from any form sexual abuse. I cannot express that enough to you.*

This all may sound quite controversial and challenging, but it will flush out any abuse going on in the home and the faster that is done the more children and young adults can begin to heal. It will be horrific to begin with, but light will end the darkness. Similarly, it will provide confidence within your children of what is okay and what is not. Then, in time, future generations will have a new understanding and know how damaging abuse is.

Child sexual abuse is also becoming more prevalent between children now too. I have recently been supporting a friend whose son was abused by a 13-year-old girl – he was nine when it came to light, although this peer-on-peer sexual abuse started when he was seven and she was 11. Unaware, my friend encouraged her son to play at his school friend's house, not knowing the elder sister was preying on him and his other friends each time they visited. Don't be fooled – child-on-child sex abuse is becoming the norm, and schools are now directed to incorporate a clause into their policies regarding peer-on-peer abuse. If this wasn't on the rise, why would schools need to have a policy about it? This is not a good direction for future generations to be heading. We must all take some responsibility now!

In my complementary therapy practice, I have also worked with young women who have experienced rape at university for example. Again, this is another area where sexual abuse is rife. I can't believe I'm even having to highlight this. These young adults have all been raised by parents. So parents, I implore you to take responsibility for educating your sons and daughters in this area and discuss it with them.

It all needs to be halted in its tracks now. Speak about it, flush it out and create a generation that knows this is all so very wrong so they in turn can teach their children, and we wipe this barbaric behaviour out. The true nature and Integrity of Love will be flowing through us as we do this – trust in that.

I was never raped, but my heart goes out deeply to any woman, man or child who has been. That said, I lived in fear of it happening daily for five years, and other stuff happened instead which I don't need to go into – suffice to say it made its mark. I have had years to process the different layers and impact abuse had on me. The breakthrough came though when I fully accepted the abuse was beyond wrong and yet it had happened. I stopped trying to fight the fact it had happened and change that it had.

I validated myself with congruency in the wrongness of the abuse, and I liberated myself in the realisation that it had happened, and it was in the past, which I therefore could not change.

This was deeply liberating and gave me the gift of coming into the present moment to reside, and let me tell you, that is blissful!

As I mentioned earlier, what goes unsaid causes the problems. This should have been spoken about more openly. Problems certainly don't arise when the true nature and Integrity of Love is fully present and not blocked. We must acknowledge these heinous actions of abuse as just that, so others do not have to weave and navigate through life with the additional scars and torment child sex abuse bestows on the one preyed upon. Parent your child/ren consciously to know it is a crime for the sake of humanity and so we can wipe out such horrors from being repeated.

Meantime, if you've ever suffered any form of sexual abuse, I want you to know you can heal. It takes courage and time. You don't have to do it alone though – there really is help out there in the form of human support as well as energetic support and ultimately the true nature and Integrity of Love can be your gift. It is possible to recover and reclaim connection with your essence. You CAN do this.

PTSD

I lived in fear and constantly on edge for around five years – the fear of being communicated with and touched inappropriately, or worse, attacked. And all the while, I did not understand how my mother could continue not to save me and move me to safety and security. Instead, for a number of those five years she knowingly continued enabling it by what I refer to as her "not doing anything". From my perspective, she chose not to believe me and not to take appropriate action early on.

Once my mother and her partner separated and he moved into new accommodation, my mother took me to his new house because she needed to discuss something with him. To this day, I have no clue regarding her rationale for taking me. However, when I was in the doorway of his new house, I froze in utter fear, but she coaxed me in to his lounge where I was briefly faced with him. They went on into the next room. What on earth she was thinking let alone doing I don't know – but she wasn't awake or conscious about her actions. What I noticed in the lounge, though, was that my mother had given the abuser belongings of mine, including a picture on the wall which had been stored in one of my bedroom drawers. She had even given him a cushion I'd made for her when I was nine. I was ragingly livid and beyond hurt. Afterwards when I asked her why she'd given him the items, she said, "To make it more like a home for him – he needed help". I had no words at this point – I was simply stunned by her response. I knew he had kept threatening suicide because she kept leaving me alone to run to him in panic and distress during those early months after what I term as our escape. It felt like I'd finally escaped the torture of living under the same roof as him like a captive and my body could begin to rest. What about the help I needed though? It wasn't given to me by my mother, I just went deeper into the darkness within and the anger sat raging internally like a burning furnace. That day of being taken to his house, post-traumatic stress disorder (PTSD) was triggered – albeit mildly compared to others. The trauma in question was not only the trauma of the abuse, but also the trauma of my mother's chaotic actions and lack of sense.

As you may imagine, over the years this flipping back into the trauma of my mother's chaotic decisions, particularly when she doesn't take appropriate action regarding family matters has caused my mind to experience a very challenging relationship with her.

Mindfulness as well as meditation have helped with this though and I'll expand on that a bit later.

Narcissism

This again is such a cruel form of manipulation and control. From my experience of having lived in the environment, I would say my mother has Narcissistic Personality Disorder (NPD). It is only in adulthood I have come to realise this. For many years I'd been hoodwinked by this behaviour type because it is dangerously subtle, but it is so gobsmackingly obvious once becoming aware of what narcissism is. It's like all the cogs are out of sync and in confusion, but that has become normalised. Then the cogs slot into place and all that has been cruel can be seen in stark white light. Or it's like a domino effect. I had the first realisation and then there was a tsunami effect as I realised more and more how manipulative and cruel it had been. It has taken me just as much, if not more, in-depth work and healing to work through this as it did to recover from the abuse – and as you may imagine, that took years to get to a place of acceptance. The only difference here is that my mother is alive and still behaving that way because that's her choice, whereas the abuser is dead.

It's a very cruel head screw. You are controlled and tweaked and manipulated like a puppet, but you don't realise that's what is going on because you're coming from a place of giving, care, kindness and Love and they are not. They are frightened and very insecure beings who totally abuse their position and power.

Interestingly in adult life I got myself into an intimate relationship with a narcissist too. He was beyond cruel in his behaviour towards me and he also knew what he was doing. He was never physical, but a total head screw. Over time I came to understand that was my comfort zone. Ladies and gentlemen, let me tell you, comfort zones can be broken. So if you are in an abusive relationship – get help and recover yourself.

Watch Bridget Jones' mother in the films and you have your narcissist example. This is in quite a comical setting though. No element of being on the receiving end of a narcissist is funny.

A really helpful resource is:

www.daughtersofnarcissisticmothers.com

although it is also applicable to sons and partners too, of course. Danu Morrigan, who set up the site, provides some excellent information and guidance to recovery and I've included here some examples of narcissistic behaviour. The majority is described in her words below and, of course, I have Danu's permission to quote her work:

Grandiose sense of self-importance – they can never be wrong, and on the rare occasion they get called out, the sulking that then follows is utterly childlike.

Lacks empathy and is unwilling to recognise or identify with the feelings and needs of others – I had a cancer scare and I had to go for scans to ensure I didn't have any form of breast cancer. When I told my mother about the scan appointment, she advised me she was due to be go to a friend's party that day and promptly asked, "Have you got someone who can go with you?" Flabbergasted (although I don't know why because I should have known better), I replied, "I could ask a friend". There she was, off the hook to continue her plans and go to the party, which she did. For me this type of behaviour she demonstrated falls into abandonment, too. In those days before the scan, I was terrified, and the one person I thought I was supposed to be able to rely on to care about me and my wellbeing within the 'love' that she has always professed to have for me, instead abandoned me.

Gaslighting – denies your sense of reality. I was constantly told, "It's not like that Carmen", yet for me as I was experiencing it, it was ABSOLUTELY like that. I'm not sure my mother will ever read this book, but I can imagine if she does, she'll say: "It wasn't like that, it wasn't that bad."

Invalidation – this forms part of gaslighting. The narcissist will dismiss and undermine your feelings and emotions to make you feel only what is acceptable to them that you feel. This ensures they can treat you in the way they want and manoeuvre the situation, so you don't get to feel the appropriate responses – it's so very cruel.

Golden child – this is the best and most wonderful child, at least in the eyes of the narcissistic. The one who she picks to be an extension of herself, and onto whom she projects all her own supposed wonderfulness. My sister has always been the golden child, can do no wrong and has repeatedly been treated preferably over me.

Ignoring – she was physically there, but not mentally, even if I had a problem. She never really paid attention unless it was to get cross and then she was very present! If I had a problem, I felt more like I was a nuisance, and on the rare occasions I did share my problems, she often did nothing. She didn't take time to talk it through with me, nor help me work it out, nor guide me. Instead I'd receive the response of either "Hmm, I'm listening", or there was silence or tears because SHE was sad – nothing about me in that little lot!

This created a couple of behaviours in me: shutdown and/or neediness. I operated between the two, fluctuating in vulnerability while simply wanting balance and peace. I remember at my 40th birthday being in a room of very specially chosen people to be there. One of my dearest friends came up to me and said, "There is so much

Love in this room for you, Carmen". I couldn't feel it – I was numb to 'Love' following years of shutdown.

The other behaviour, neediness, makes me cringe a bit because even in adulthood, on many occasions I was like that child in the class busting a gut with their hand in the air saying me, me, me, please pick me to answer the question! I can sort of smile about it as I understand at core I just craved acknowledgement that I was valid and Loved in the true sense. I simply just wanted to live in a loving and supportive environment that was calm and where I could be peaceful and joyful. Was that too much to ask?

Strings attached – there's always an angle or agenda. So, for example, if she is generous, you can be sure there are strings attached. Usually the string is to instil guilt in you or a sense of being beholden to them. For a lot of my life, well until the penny dropped my mother has NPD, I always felt like she had me on the end of invisible strings but couldn't understand why. Every time I branched out, that tug would happen and I would retreat, pulled back under control and into guilt as if I was on the end of a magnet and its force was stronger than mine.

Infantilisation – keeping the adult daughter young and dependent on them. This is so they will never be left, and so the daughter will never have her own life.

I had wanted to move to Bath when I was 16 (when she had no partner) and take an HND course in window design – a creativeness flowed through me and I know I would have been successful at it. However, in her fear and terror she told me I "wasn't strong enough to move and live away". Realising in the moment she wasn't strong enough to let me go because we weren't long out of escaping the sexual abuse situation and, being the nature I was, I chose not to put her further into pain. The pain on her face was too much for me to bear.

I stayed living with my mother, I went to Sixth Form College and failed my A-levels spectacularly instead. Then over the years, as if to rub salt in the wound, she has subsequently said I should have progressed my creative and artistic talents. Every cell in my being used to burn with anger, but now they don't, because healing from a narcissist is possible too.

My mother did encourage me to move away from our home town when it was right for her and so I did, but she hadn't equipped me for womanhood because she kept me infantilised. By now she also had a new partner, so I wasn't needed much. Incidentally, she chose another alcoholic.

Narcissistic supply – this is the constant attention they need. Phone calls were never about me and even if I did share my difficulties they were met with silence or the usual "Hmm – I'm listening" and that was it. I would be left hanging in my pain yet again.

Question: *Ask yourself as a parent, do you impact your child/ren with any of these behaviours and if you answer "Oh that's not me at all" ask yourself again from your true heart. The person who says "that couldn't possibly be me" is likely to be more of a narcissist than most.*

Action: *View Danu's website Daughters of Narcissistic Mothers and stand in the shoes of your daughter/son/partner as you read it questioning yourself on the behaviours. If you do have any of the tendencies, seek help and communicate about it. Be willing to change. It is possible and will be healing for more than just you.*

Question: *As for yourself, might you have suffered these behaviours as a daughter/son/partner of a narcissist?*

Action: *Read Danu's book You're Not Crazy It's Your Mother and also seek support as you transition through the realisations.*

It can be easy to fall into the angry blame trap during transition which is why I encourage you to get professional support on this part of your journey. Blaming others doesn't lead to peace and nor does it incorporate the true nature and Integrity of Love, hence I'm just highlighting this red flag in the hope that it serves to save you time and pain as you heal.

No empathy

Empathy can be described as:

> *The ability to identify with or understand the perspective, experiences, or motivations of another individual and to comprehend and share another individual's emotional state.*

Neither my mother nor sister seem to comprehend this and therefore nor do they seem to have the capability of bringing empathy in its full sense to our family unit.

It seems I grew up in an environment where this quality was missing, yet I know I have always been an empath; for me it's a most natural state of being. This doesn't mean I'm making anyone wrong here, I'm just highlighting how difficult that was for me – always giving and rarely receiving what I needed. I learned how not to receive … even the true nature and Integrity of Love. I shut down to it and became numb to it. I still find it difficult to receive naturally.

Giving what you want to others, for example helping them out with shopping, is not empathy – that is doing what you can or want to help them, which absolutely has its place, don't get me wrong. However, standing in the shoes of the other person and being willing and able to experience their pain or difficulty, while holding the space of Love for them as you support them through their pain or difficulty to the other side, that is empathy. Of course, that other person has to be willing to heal and receive support in the process too.

Lack of closeness

When my parents created the family unit, they were young. When they got married my dad was 21 and mum was 19. When they divorced my dad was about 27 and my mum 25. As individuals though they have not seemed to have had the capability or desire to create close bonds with my sister and I as we've grown either. This has been despite my wishes and many attempts in many different ways. I have found this so difficult to comprehend, when they were the ones who had supposedly 'in love' created us. They are oblivious though and seem to have just wanted to move forward in their lives in the way that suits them as individuals, not in a connected way at all.

Unity as we know links to Integrity.

Selfishness

This seems to be on the increase in wider parts of society. Lack of consideration for others seems to run inherently through various members of my immediate family too. I have often wondered, why aren't they fully considering all those who will be affected in this? Why are they simply putting their own immediate needs in the pot and not even communicating about it with those who will also be affected by their actions, decisions and behaviours, and instead just imposing them?

I see this more and more when observing the world of 'I' that seems to have become so fundamental to the human species these days.

Selfishness is principally self-focused, yet it is so easy to open our minds and hearts to be inclusive in our thoughts and actions. It means thinking of others equally and indiscriminately – it is the mind of we instead of just I or me. It is a compassionate mind.

Question: *I am very familiar with what it is like to be on the end of selfishness, are you? Or are you selfish?*

Question: *Have you contemplated that we are all connected and affect each other, like cells in a human body? Rogue cells cause dis-ease. Healthy cells do not, they do their job for the benefit of the human being as a whole; in other words, they work from a place of Integrity.*

Action: *List five times in the last week you've made a decision that affects someone else, yet you have selfishly got on with it anyway without a thought for what the true nature and Integrity of Love would do in such circumstances.*

Question: *What reasons arise in the answers and to how many can you apply the word 'selfish' or simply "I wanted it/to regardless of others"?*

Question: *Why is that okay and is that what the true nature and Integrity of Love would do?*

Question: *What can you do to reduce your level of selfishness? By the way, don't be fooled by your ego that you're not selfish because we all are at times.*

Action: *Contemplate how often you truly teach your child/ren to put others first unconditionally.*

Action: *Let us raise the level of true GIVING, especially to the earth. Contemplate how else you can give to the earth without taking anything in return, and then take that action.*

Action: *Perhaps go into a charity environment on your own or with your child/ren where you must think of others and simply give of yourselves and care about others in the first instance. Don't ask for something in return, such as sponsorship money, and don't give your children pocket money for doing it but find something you and they can simply give to. An example would be a community garden or litter pick in your community or an animal sanctuary. There are so many opportunities to volunteer for the benefit of others.*

Cherish others and the feeling you will have is pure connection to the true nature and Integrity of Love.

Lack of communication

Clearly our fractured family is actually more than fractured.

I haven't been asked what I have needed as a member in my family and it be given to or shared with me, except on the very odd occasion – I can probably count on one hand how many times I've requested help. One of these times was a very low point in my life and my sister did ask what she could do from Australia. I requested a little more contact with my nephews so as to create connection and relationships with them via a short Skype call every other week. She allowed this for a couple of months and then withdrew the option saying she was too busy and it was too difficult. My sister was jealous again, I could see it. She didn't like the bonds that were forming and the Love my nephews and I were experiencing and sharing, I could see that very plainly.

I don't have a relationship with my dad because he doesn't want communication with me. I have tried on three occasions to resurrect some form of communication with him after our relationship broke down. I received a one sentence reply to the first attempt. I asked him how he was and told him I'd been thinking of him. He replied, "I'm fine, thank you" and that was pretty much it. I was hit with silence on the second two attempts.

A number of years later we were at the same event for my aunt's birthday. My dad, his wife, my youngest brother and his partner were all sitting at a table together as I walked into the venue. I stood at the bar with the cousins I'd walked in with, desperately hoping my dad would be the adult for once and come over to me and break the ice. He didn't. After about 20 minutes all my immediate family members got up from the table where they had been sitting and they walked towards the buffet table which was just behind where I was standing. Not one of them spoke as they passed me. I turned my back on them in that moment. Not flowing in the true nature and Integrity of Love at all. I was hurting and breaking inside – the child in me was present that evening, not the adult that was physically standing there. Yet the outer me was putting on the performance of getting on with it and presenting the façade I'd learned to bring out when needed. My protection armour was well and truly on. How much was I kidding myself? How can a façade on the outside possibly help a breaking heart on the inside? What it needed was Integrity and Love.

Whenever I visited my dad as a teenager and even as young woman in my 20s and 30s, it was the child who still needed her daddy that turned up and she never really was able to get close to him. I hadn't been able to get close to him since that moment on the side of the lake. Ahead of me in the love stakes was the new wife, his two sons and my sister. My dad and his wife then adopted their two nieces and nephew following devastatingly unfortunate circumstances and it was lovely of my dad and his wife to do this, I don't deny that at all.

The impact on me though was that I felt pushed even further down the priority list. It was like I was treading water in a deep sea, and in front of me but out of reach they were all on the raft with him and they were even waving at me. Not noticing, let alone caring about the deep suffering I was experiencing as it felt like I was constantly almost drowning in the lack of so much. That's how it felt as a child and as a young woman. These are examples of imprints that can form when the true nature and Integrity of Love are not present.

On one of my 'holiday visits' my dad was telling me about a birthday celebration he'd had. He was waxing lyrical about how wonderful it had been that all his friends had made it and ALL the family had been there, so he was with everyone who was important to him and it was one of the best days of his life. I didn't receive an invitation to that party. I just sat in front of him going further into numbness, as he reminisced oblivious to my pain.

Where my mother is concerned, communication is not her forte either as you can probably gather by now. If I have tried to engage her in discussion to heal family matters, she either goes silent saying occasionally "I'm listening" or she cries. There is no give. So when we are in contact we talk about the weather and what she and her friends are up to. She will ask if I'm ok, to which I always now say yes, and so life continues. Lack of communication can cause so much chaos for young minds as does being too busy or apathetic.

So, I kindly ask you to notice the pain of others and don't avoid it because it's difficult for you to deal with, or because you're too busy to deal with it. I also ask that you notice your own pain and face it, so it can leave you. Pain can be dissolved far more easily immediately after it happens, don't waste those precious moments, be conscious, make time and allow healing as you pause and allow the true nature and Integrity of Love to flow through you.

Action: *Have courage, give clarity, gentle honesty and openness while holding a space of loving kindness as this does not cause chaos.*

One of my clients recently told me about how he organises a weekend away with his children individually. They go separately – just dad and child together. The child gets to choose where they go and they simply spend time together connecting, going places, doing stuff, chatting and having fun. He wants to do this especially as now they are spending less time together as the children become more and more independent. The children are currently 9 and 13 and at this age could easily start to lose connection with their parents, but with such thought it's more likely they will remain close. What lucky children and what thoughtful parenting. It was beautiful to hear this. Communication is vital for cohesion.

Question: *When was the last time you fully connected with your child for more than 10 minutes at a time, and I also mean the child inside your adult daughter or son – the imprinted one?*

Question: *What stops you doing this more regularly if you aren't doing it?*

Question: *Is the reason(s) that stops you more important than the flow of the true nature and Integrity of Love between you and your child?*

Action: *Have courage and try to establish contact with your child and adult child if you have become estranged and keep trying as long as you have breath in your body. The child may well 'kick back' in their behaviour, but it won't last long in the grand scheme of life.*

Action: *Don't let your pride defeat you. Allow the rift to heal and come up with solutions agreeable to you both. Let the possibility of the true nature and Integrity of Love encapsulate and guide you.*

Question: *When was the last time you fully connected with yourself and listened to what your internal beingness is trying to tell you? Let it arise and with consistent practice you can come into being comfortable with what you find and heal.*

Little responsibility

I'm sure you will realise this was something else pretty much lacking in my family unit. Crikey, I'm sounding like a broken record, aren't I?!

My father gone and on his way creating and providing for his 'new' family. Paying maintenance until I was 16, my holiday visits to him and phone calls, and giving me a deposit for my first property (which I had to request) doesn't really cut it. In my view there is much more to being a father than that, but he hasn't wanted to be that type of father to me, so I choose to let it go.

I understand my mother was doing her best in those early years, while also working and being in the midst of dealing emotionally, mentally and physically with the death of her father and her son, and with my dad's decision and choice to leave our family unit to be with another woman. She did the best she could with the resources she had available to her, perhaps to the point of overload and I have never underestimated that. My sense is that through the fogginess and haze of all that torture, ensuring that we had a roof over our heads, that we were clean, and that food was put on our table was as much as she could do while treading water in the ocean of despair, and I hold great heart for her in that regard.

Not surprisingly, I suspect my mother must have burned out in those early years, but she has stuck there and hasn't recovered herself. There has been little in the form of her taking responsibility for her actions or recovery over the last 35 years from what I've observed and experienced; in fact, I have often felt like I'm the mother and she has allowed that.

Little remorse and inability to apologise

Apologising can be difficult for some, and, you guessed it, especially in my family. I can probably count on my hand the number of apologies I've received from them in my life – and that's from all of them!

Not once has my father indicated he has felt any remorse for leaving me behind – all he has said is that he "couldn't be the father I wanted him to be". Yet neither has he ever asked me once, what I wanted him to be or have needed of him as my father. My mother has simply asked for forgiveness for the situation regarding the sexual abuse, which I gave her, and then she continued in her narcissistic form, and not once asking what I need and then providing it.

Even when I have expressed to my mother the abhorrence of her actions towards me and what would help me, this is simply met with silence. It is as if she doesn't admit to those actions, let alone acknowledge them, then they cannot have occurred. No acknowledgement, no apology, no remorse, just the requirement from her that I continue to feed her narcissistic supply. Nor from my sister. Nothing except justification for her own behaviour and utterly vile accusations directed at me, which don't match what has been in my heart.

I find it so baffling because, with Love in the heart, apologising and expressing genuine remorse is so easy – I simply don't understand why people resist it. It can clear so much tension, angst and energy if done with honest communication and deep sincerity, and if those you are giving your apology to are willing to accept it in the good faith it is given. Behaviours can then change and more peace can arise.

I remember when my mother was going to see my sister in Australia for a six-week visit and before she flew I requested that she ask my sister what I had done to her that was so bad our relationship was in such a state, and that perhaps we could look to resolve it? My sister was blocking me at that time. On my mother's return, I asked her what my sister's reply was. My mother confessed that "There was no time to have that conversation – they'd been so busy."

Is it any wonder our family is so fractured?

Question: *Is there something you could sincerely apologise for now?*

Action: *If there is, do it and expect nothing in return. The apology is something you give unconditionally and with the true nature and Integrity of Love in mind. It is a bonus and, of course, beneficial for all if matters resolve as a result of your apology and peace for both parties arises, but if you expect that, you may end up being disappointed and that may bring even more suffering in the mind.*

Little time, energy and willingness to understand

Lack of time, energy and understanding of how to engage with the soul and essence of the child in front of them in the moment was prevalent. My soul and essence were there in front of their bare eyes, but it rarely felt like either of them saw it.

Lack of openness and honesty

As I mentioned earlier, what goes unsaid causes the problems. Openness and honesty are paramount for healthy relating, and I believe it is far easier in the long run for all concerned to have matters discussed in an open manner, while holding the space in the energy of loving kindness. Discussions can be guided towards a conclusion and solution so all feel heard and can be at peace with decisions, thus preventing confusion.

Clearly there isn't any of this in my family to this day.

Honesty = Integrity

Sweeping things under the carpet, or ostrich behaviour as I call it, serves only to cause confusion, lengthen pain and drive wedges between people.

Question: *How honest and open are you in your family environment?*

Question: *What are you sweeping under the carpet in the hope that it will go away or it's just a bit tricky to deal with right now, but deep down you know it will only raise its ugly head in the future?*

Question: *What are you afraid of?*

Question: *Why are you choosing to avoid being honest and open?*

Action: *Read the section on Fear later in this book and come to understand Fear = drama and story. Fear can be termed as an illusion.*

Action: *Contemplate how you can create a more healthily open and honest environment for your family.*

Action: *Repeat the same question and do the same action regarding your intimate relationship, your working environment and also for your friendship groups.*

We take offence way too often, we fight, we argue, we go silent, we seethe inside, yet how often do we think "What would the true nature and Integrity of Love do right now?" and then do that. How often do we give others the chance to be honest and open without passing judgement on them, and how often are we ourselves truly open and honest while holding a space for the true nature and Integrity of Love to flow?

Question: *How often are you truly open and honest with yourself?*

Question: *By not being honest and open are you causing more harm?*

Please bear in mind, I am not talking of direct, blunt, unkind, brutal honesty, the things that are sometimes best left unsaid, because these do exist too, of course. I am talking of honesty that has the wish for healing and peace behind it.

Question: *Could you be more honest and open while holding a space for the true nature and Integrity of Love to flow as you open and become more honest with yourself and others?*

By the way – this can take practice, so start with small irritations rather than the really deep and big stuff you may wish to work on. You can build up to that with practice.

Question: *How vulnerable and authentic are you allowing yourself to be with yourself?*

Action: *Hold a space of loving kindness for yourself and allow yourself to sit with yourself. No phones, no music, no TV, no other being. Just sit with yourself and be. Do this for 10 minutes every day and come to know your essence.*

Question: *What does your heart truly desire?*

Action: *Hold a space of loving kindness and write out a list of what your heart desires – and be truly honest, don't let fear distract you either, you are only writing a list at this point after all.*

"Vulnerability is my strength." – Diana Cooper

Example: You wish to drink less alcohol, but don't know how. The first step is acknowledging you've been open and honest with yourself about this. The next step might be sharing that with your partner and asking for their support as you work out how you go about turning your desire into action. If you don't have a partner it might be a trusted friend or doctor that you speak to.

Example: You want to be in a relationship, but your pride and hurt from previous relationships means you've put up a wall and a bravado to shield your pain. Ask yourself: "What would Love do?" if you said this to Love. Love would say, "Don't be afraid, be gentle with yourself, have courage and be open to it, you have my support."

Be kind and gentle with yourself in this process too.

You may find you've included more 'things' on your list of heart desires rather than behaviours/actions/feelings.

Action: *Contemplate how many 'things' are on the list as opposed to 'feelings' – for example, a new handbag, new pair of trainers, another iPad versus less arguing, more peace, more Love. Delete the 'things' at this point and concentrate on the internal desires.*

Too much future and past, and not enough present

My mother brought us up pretty much single-handed and she never took a penny from the state. I have great respect for her in many ways for that and much to thank her for too, including that she gave me life, and she also taught me to think of others and put them first, although I think this went a little out of balance along the way.

My mother wasn't ever really present though, and still isn't often when I'm in her company. She's a complex character, suffering her own journey and imprints from her own childhood. Her mother had apparently been given electric shock treatment back in the day and was on prescription Valium. I know my mother suffered at the hands of her mother too – having scissors put to her throat at one point. I often wonder if that is why she goes silent when challenged. I also often wonder what imprints my grandmother must have taken to heart as a child for her wellbeing to reach such a low as well. These are just some of the reasons I asked you to suspend your judgements of my family members at the start of this book.

By her own admission though, my mother is always busy and much of this has been so she hasn't had to think, which in essence means confront and heal her pain. So she distracts herself keeping herself busy, and yet her mind can't help wandering, even within the distraction. I have watched her deep in pain thinking she's distracting herself by busying herself. I have tried in so many ways to help her over the years, supporting her to have courage to clear inwards, but she just won't. That is her prerogative, and I now accept it.

What lack of presence does though is gently push the child away with a "What's the point?" attitude. My mother wasn't always busy working, managing a home and us. She also distracted herself with other people's problems and she socialised a lot too – I remember it well because I just wanted her to sit on the sofa with me and be – that's all, simple moments of togetherness and being connected at the heart. Time to smile at each other, tell jokes, laugh, seek advice and just share being together. On the rare occasion she did sit down in the evening on the sofa even just to watch the TV, she'd be asleep within 10 minutes. I'd sigh with sadness inside seeing her tiredness and just wishing with all my heart it didn't have to be that way.

In later life, I remember my mother looking lovingly at my three-year-old nephew and then turning to me saying "He'll be something one day". In that moment every cell of me burned with pain as I couldn't believe what I was hearing! So I blurted out "He IS someone right now!" He was there, standing in the true nature and Integrity of Love, our hearts meeting, yet she missed it completely because she was off out there in the future.

As for my father – well, he simply just wasn't present because he was off creating his new life and in reality he didn't look back.

I don't ever remember a family member saying, "Are you okay, Carmen? What can I do to help you? Do you need anything? Shall we talk it through and take time to do that? We can sort this together."

How could anyone not notice that I'd been interfered with and the fear I was living in on a daily basis? How could anyone not see my pain and want to help me heal from it? Surely if they were present enough they would have noticed?

When I have described presence while teaching workshops, at the point I say, "The best gift you can give someone is presence in your moments together", I can see the faces in front of me melt. It's as though everyone there knows what that would mean to them at their heart and either that melts them, or it is the thought of giving that same feeling of presence to someone else. Either way, they are feeling the true nature and Integrity of Love.

Action: *If you are struggling to be present, learn how to be. There are plenty of mindfulness courses around and if you can't get out find some resources online or get a book. I recommend mostly The Power of Now by Eckhart Tolle – this is a great starting point while containing deep wisdom and beauty.*

Question: *What does being present with someone else mean to you and them?*

Question: *What is it like being present with yourself?*

Question: *Ask yourself, how often each day am I truly present in the company of my parents, child/ren, siblings, partner, friends? Also consider, when you're on the phone, Facetime, Skype, in person, etc.*

Question: *For what purpose do I choose not to be present?*

Action: *Train in mindfulness and/or meditation for example.*

Action: *Practice holding the space for the other person to simply be without judging them in any way.*

Action: *Don't be waiting to speak when the other person is. Instead, listen to their words and what they are saying.*

Action: *Learn how to be more often with the essence of the being you are with, not your chattering mind, but their essence and ask them to be more often with your true essence.*

Action: *Be there in your core essence too.*

The now is all we have. The past cannot be changed and yesterdays cannot return. The past can only be learned from, so why keep revisiting it once you acknowledge the learnings? The future cannot be known, so why worry about it? That is then, this is now. The present is a set of causes and conditions coming together and our response to them. We can always respond with the true nature and Integrity of Love in our hearts. We just need to become conscious to it, have the will, practice doing it and discipline our minds to not deviate from this practice.

Confusion

Such chaotic environments for children growing up cause high degrees of confusion and anxiety. It seemed almost everyone on the outside of our family thought my mother remarkable for bringing up such 'beautiful' children, having been left by my father, and they could see how much our mother loved us. By that virtue, they were implying clearly my father didn't. I used to feel sick to my stomach as I heard her praised by friends and she preened her ego. Love us? In her way perhaps she did and still does, but it didn't and doesn't feel like what I understand as Love or unconditional kindness.

What was going on behind closed doors was utter despair and head screw confusion as I developed in an environment of an alcoholic paedophile, a father who didn't know and simply didn't care enough to honour his role of father, a narcissistic mother and a bitterly cruel sister.

All the while, I just wanted peace inside, to escape the horror and to be Loved – truly Loved.

I once observed a father of a child in a newly divorced family situation and thought him so caring and deeply present for his 12-year-old son. At bed time, he let his son get himself into bed and said, "Think of your three things and I'll be up". After about 10 minutes he went upstairs to comfort his son to sleep and they spent about 10 to 15 minutes talking through these three questions:

- What is great that has happened today?
- What concerns have you had today?
- How can we solve them together in these moments?

They did this every evening his son was with him. It could be argued that this can now be done every evening whether you're with your child or not, what with all the technology available these days.

I still melt inside (which is what it sometimes feels like for me when the true nature and Integrity of Love flows) as I recall this, as it was such a thoughtful, caring and loving exercise to carry out. That father and son probably shared in moments of deep pain together, but they will also have healed through it strongly together too. It just takes a little bit of courage, honesty, time and the presence to ensure confusion doesn't take over. I ask you to really pause here and be deeply honest.

Question: *Is there confusion in your child's mind about anything?*

Question: *What can you do to alleviate any confusion present?*

Action: *Take action appropriate to the confusion and help lift it away so it can dissolve, and in its place relief, peace and joy can arise.*

Lack of caring guidance for the individual

Each child is an individual and, I believe, deserves equal amount of focus, attention and energy, in accordance with their individual essence. As an example, a relation of mine had a baby boy and he immediately became the centre of their world. He received the best of everything and a lot of focus was placed on him. A couple of years later they also had a daughter and life suddenly got a whole lot busier for this family. A year or so later, I found it hard to hear that the daughter didn't experience as much as the son had during his first year – for example, going to swimming lessons – simply because there wasn't time. This is the 'fitting in' scenario I often found myself in as a child. I don't see how it is fair on the second child; energetically it is felt, there is a feeling of being lesser. I can only talk from the perspective of being a second child and having talked to other second-born children plus witnessing scenarios like the one described here. I guess at core what I am highlighting is the importance of being present to this, of giving equally to all your children, whatever their (birth order) position in the family, while holding each individual essence at heart.

Question: *Do you put equal effort into all of your children and if not, for what purpose do you choose not to? Be honest in your heart when you answer; no ifs, no buts, no justification, just answer honestly.*

Question: *Why for example, is it okay not to put the same effort into the second or third and fourth child as you did your first?*

Action: *Stand in the shoes of the first child and feel what it is to know you have received more of your parent's focus and attention – how does that feel? Energetically, it is also felt by the other child/ren, believe me.*

Question: *Do you treat each of your children with the individuality that they possess or do you clump your children together in a kind of one-size-fits-all approach?*

Action: *If you have a child/ren – experience their essence, know it and nurture it into full blossom. Do not hamper them by moulding them into what you never achieved, and do not be too busy to know their true core essence as it expands.*

As an example, I remember when it came to the time of choosing my options for 'O' levels – that's GCSEs these days! I was told that I had to do physics and chemistry because that's what my older sister had done. I was utterly useless at science, but we had to take a science subject and inside me I had an inkling I'd like to study biology. However, I'd heard that there was a rat dissection involved in the course at some point so abolished the thought of biology, based on the cruelty involved in that one lesson and my fear of it. In truth, I would have liked to study biology. Instead though, I argued I should just be taking general science.

If I could speak to my 14-year-old self now I'd say, "Don't be fearful, just take biology. You do not agree with the dissection and its unnecessariness, but it is just one lesson and you can avoid it. Your mother won't support you and write a letter, but you can eloquently explain why you're not comfortable doing the dissection and so avoid it. The rest of it will be fascinating and you'll love it."

So where were my parents at that point, because I don't have any recollection of a meaningful conversation around why wasn't I considering biology in full? Oh yes. They were in their own heads still playing out their silent war interspersed with arguments down the phone, after which the tension was palpable yet again! Needless to say, I failed chemistry dismally and I didn't do much better in physics either because my mind doesn't work in that way.

Question: *Are you in the midst of a silent war with your ex? If so, for what purpose and how do you think it benefits your child/ren? Stand in their shoes for a moment and feel the tension they are caught between.*

Question: *Is your ego or pride ruling your behaviour when surely there would be more benefit from allowing the true nature and Integrity of Love to flow through you and into your situation?*

Question: *Do you think you're a better parent than your ex? Can you drop this judgement?*

Action: *Take a first step, be courageous and let go of any 'words' that may fly back in your face from ex - they are only words after all. Hold the intention for peace to arise and, slowly or even more quickly than you can hope for, peace can be given the opportunity to arise and your child/ren will not have to exist within tension, but shared care and guidance from the two people who created the child/ren in Love, right?*

If you need third party help, get it for all your sakes and the sake of your children's children.

Question: *Are you guiding your children as individuals?*

Question: *Do you know what the essence of your child is?*

Question: *Do you indeed know what your own essence is?*

A couple of years ago, Lynda, a family friend who is more like family to me than my birth family, relayed a story from my childhood. I had no recollection of this scenario, but she clearly remembers it as if it were yesterday; here it is.

We went to her family home every other Sunday for roast dinner during the winter months. This was quite a joy for me as it felt like a true family environment. There were also people taking a safe interest in me, and togetherness was tangible, so it felt like a family ought to in my tiny little mind. One of those days, Lynda's dog Hamish, a bit of a grumpy West Highland terrier, was barking at me and, apparently, I turned to him and in no uncertain terms said, "Hamish, why are you barking at me when I Love you so much?!" I can imagine my utter confusion, as this pretty much sums up my confusion regarding humans too. I share in Love and they just abuse it! At core, we are all Love and we have the ability to Love all beings, but instead we choose to 'bark' at each other in the form of judgement, resentment, bitterness, jealousy, anger, blame, shame, violence, fear, and so on. Instead, we have the ability to create thoughts of kindness, peacefulness, thoughtfulness, joy, encouragement and happiness for our fellow beings. So why do we choose the former? Start your day with "What would the Integrity of Love do?"

Part 4:
The Pain and Knock-on Effects

As I grew and developed in the environment I was born into – the shaky foundations and where others' wants were more important than, not even equal to, my own – their wants and needs became so ingrained in me, I could not shine through and I lost my way.

Once I became aware though, I began the process of unlearning those habitual thought processes, behaviours and actions which belonged to someone else and instead allowed the revival of what seemed right in my heart and congruent with my essence.

I was fought at every turn though. For example, my mother told me to get a 'proper job' when I started my complementary therapy practice. I was 30 at the time. Needless to say, I carried on being from my heart and even today I am a complementary therapist. I'm so pleased part of my essence is a feisty warrior!

So let's look at the damaging knock-on effects of growing from a child to an adult in my family:

- Pain
- Sadness
- Being left with others
- Having to "fit in"
- Chaos and complication
- Being on the end of much jealousy, bullying and manipulation
- Separateness
- Lack of confidence
- Lowering self-esteem
- Neediness
- Treading water
- Fear
- Anger
- Insecurity
- Too much identification
- Perfectionism
- The incessant need to fix things / make it okay for others

- Growing in the wrong direction – not allowed to be who I am but who I'd been brought up to be
- More abuse and patterns repeating
- Confusion and lack of confidence within relationships
- Abortion
- Burnout twice
- Brokenness
- Aloneness
- Suicidal thoughts
- Struggle
- Blame
- Guilt and remorse
- Lack of trust
- Shame

Pain

The word 'pain' has its roots in the Latin word poena, meaning 'penalty'. Realising this helps me remember the pain I am experiencing is just my Karma, i.e. the causes and conditions coming together relating to my previous thoughts and actions. This may not resonate for everyone, but it now helps deter me from going into thoughts of blaming others for what is arising.

Often pain has sat inside me – just there – a sorrowfulness from my childhood. A darkness like the inside of a cave on a winter day – cold, damp, musty and dark. However, as I have purified through the layers of energy of my system, that darkness dissipates, and the light flows more easily. Joy arises sweetly and peacefully and for me this feels like I'm merged more with the true nature and Integrity of Love, the more I move along my path.

It can, of course, simply be done with mind too. If I think of and come from the place of the true nature and Integrity of Love I lift, and a flow simply enters my being like from a bottomless well at my heart centre.

Whichever way I work, it can help to hold in mind "I start again with beginner mind". This does not of course mean to behave recklessly and then simply begin again. Here, I intend it to relate to kindness for the self and others. We can catch ourselves, pause, breathe, be kind in that moment asking: "What would the true nature and Integrity of Love do?" and then carry that forward in our behaviour, actions and thoughts.

This includes kindness to self as well as others of course, which helps those of us who have been or currently display 'doormat behaviour'. It helps us keep ourselves equal, which we all are.

Despite forgiving my mother many things, a few years ago she managed to hit an all-time high with her lack of thought, compassion, and Love. After much consideration I decided to go 'no contact' with her. I contemplated this deeply before doing so, including the question of how I would feel if she died during the time I was implementing the 'no contact'. I will be very honest with you as I have been throughout this book. I concluded that I was so beaten numb mentally and emotionally from the abuse in her behaviour towards me that I would actually be okay should she pass away during my silence. This took time to contemplate – I had to go deep within. Once I'd considered it fully from all angles, I wrote explaining that for the sake of my mental health and wellbeing I was going 'no contact'. I remember feeling the experience of utter freedom like the moment in the film *Twelve Years A Slave*, when Solomon walked out of the field and physically got free from his captor. Like him, I had got away too, and a huge weight lifted from my shoulders and from within my heart.

Interestingly, after a year my mother thought I'd had long enough being silent and got in touch because she was visiting my cousin who doesn't live far from me. I was actually in a very good place by then, but I would have also been quite happy to remain 'no contact' full stop. During that year of silence, I had also experienced burnout and had chosen to leave my job in the corporate world. It was as though I'd reached peak trauma and my bodymind had been fully broken open in order that I could rebuild from my essence and this time on my terms. What followed was a lot of deep searching and purifying within my being. I was limp in body, mind and spirit and it was an excruciatingly painful and exhausting time – I had been cracked properly open. Gradually I came to a place of forgiveness again though, and so went along to meet my mother.

I remember sitting opposite her in a coffee shop where we agreed to meet, and during the conversation I calmly said, "You are no less than me and no more than me, and I am no less than you and no more than you, we are equal." She fizzed inside from the depths of her soul – I watched her whole being as it rose from inside to show on her face – the lack of control she now had over me. She didn't say a word, so I continued: "If there is to be any way forward you will need to understand that". Again, she didn't say a word, but that didn't matter now, because those were the parameters for our relationship and I had set them.

For about a year we gently went along and there seemed to be a little more understanding between us. So then I set about inviting my sister to come to the table too, so we could all heal for the sake of each of us as individuals as well as in unity. Put the past behind us, draw a line in the sand and begin again in gentleness and kindness for each other. Peace.

My sister found this too difficult and could not come to the table in peace, and of course my mother couldn't help herself and the narcissism took over. Her Golden Child can do no wrong and she also watched from the side lines doing nothing to contribute to bringing our family into unity. As you can imagine, her doing nothing triggered PTSD reactions within me and, yes, I had more inner work to do!

The following spring, I heard out of the blue and by total accident that between my mother, step-father, my sister with her family, and a couple of other life-long family friends, they had between them hired two cottages for a 'family' holiday in France that summer. I did not get an invitation and the reason given by my mother was: "You and Elise don't get on, what am I supposed to do?" The depth of pain I felt at that point was like glass being scratched with a knife and the numbness returned straight away where they are all concerned. For the best part of seven years, but particularly those latter two years, I'd done my utmost to bring our family together to begin again in peace.

Accepting my sister's antics, my mother's abstinence and lack of contribution, and tirelessly making every effort I possibly could to bring in peace, as well as keeping my heart open … well, it was a tough path to tread and I had reached my limit for the time being. I implemented 'no contact' again with my mother. It didn't feel like the true nature and Integrity of Love was flowing but I needed to invite Love for me at that point until I could get strong again. My inner pain was playing more strongly than my inner peace. However, I didn't judge myself, but instead allowed time for the game inside me to settle and dissipate. It is important we allow ourselves to be not perfect on such a journey, although at all times we have to watch our Integrity like a hawk. I can unequivocally in wholeness say:

I'm not judging myself but allowing the game inside me to settle as I observe the pain rising, falling and retreating – I trust the pain too will pass.

Therefore, I know I am in Integrity, and when I have clarity and it feels pure and I come out of the darkness, I can take action from that place, but until then it is beneficial for me to keep my distance.

In his writings, Jason Garner talks about "allowing our humanness", which can be helpful to remember at tricky points along the path. We're not Buddhas or Gods capable of divine forgiveness, for instance. What we can do is learn to be at peace with what we find, not constantly track peace as though it's off out in the distance at the top of the mountain. In this instance, I am at peace being in 'no contact'. My mother probably isn't, and until she stops her internal fight and I mine, this will most likely be the case.

Question: *What is your pain?*

Action: *Once the actual pain is acknowledged, then the healing can begin and you can work through this yourself, or with help of course. The key is to ask direct questions of the self while holding a space of loving kindness, acceptance of what is. Allow yourself to be the whole of you as you sit with yourself or a therapist or friend or partner and allow the questions and answers to arise.*

Action: *If you have children, you can gently do this with them too, when they are in pain. Even simple pain like when they fall over and graze their knee. Don't be in a rush to gloss over it, distract them, quickly shove a plaster on it and that makes it better. Perhaps simply hold a space of loving kindness for them to feel their pain, acknowledge what it is they tell you, soothe their pain so they can then gently move on with peace in their being.*

Recently I witnessed two people discussing their individual pains with one person comparing her pain to his pain. The lady was suffering from losing her son six years previously, the man was referring to the pain from abuse. The conversation was highlighting that strength, stamina and resilience are needed to come into our power. Yet if the true nature and Integrity of Love were encouraged to be present in the first place, why would we need such strength, stamina and resilience? We would be able to reside in the safety of Love naturally, peacefully and joyfully would we not?

Question: *Do you see how humans in general are devoid of the true nature and Integrity of Love?*

These are totally different forms of pain and the healing required would be very different and therefore should not be compared. Yes, pain is pain and simply overwhelming at times. Healing from loss of a loved one will be a totally different process from healing abuse though.

How one person recovers from their pain will be different from how another person does, even if they both were abused for instance, and this should be respected so all can heal. We are all on our own path.

"Pain can leave us once we have learned all we need to know of the experience." - Anon

One of the most powerful gifts I believe we can give another, is to listen in the moment to that other, without judgement, just holding the space of loving kindness. Let the other be heard. Acknowledge their pain. The same can be said for ourselves. We can give that gift to ourselves too. Listen in the moment to what is going on inside, without judgement, just holding the space of loving kindness. Hear what it is, feel what is arising and allow it to surface so it can then dissipate.

If you wish, you can follow this seven-step format for each pain, whether physical, mental, emotional or spiritual.

1. Slow down and pause/stop … and breathe
2. Hold the space of loving kindness … and breathe
3. Notice the pain inside your being, look at it from all angles … and breathe
4. Allow all that arises in that moment – allowing it just to be, not trying to manipulate it into something it isn't. Letting it be in that space of the true nature and Integrity of Love … and breathe
5. Acknowledge the pain and discuss it if required and allow solutions to arise … and breathe
6. Allow the pain to dissipate … and breathe
7. Move on with peace in your being … and breathe

Sadness

The sadness or even sorrowfulness that resided in me for years was so deep in my soul. I have looked at photos of me while growing up and in those images it is not a happy child I see, but a timid, nervous, unsure, unconfident, shy, sensitive and unhappy being forcing herself in life.

I understand now that I also took on a lot of my mother's sadness. People who are grieving can create an air of depressive energy around them and when you're immersed in it, without knowing it can be easy to fuse with it too.

So when people say, "Children are resilient, they'll get on with it", I want to puke and I want to scream from the rooftops, "Children are NOT resilient, but they will get on with it, they have to when others impose their shit on them and they are under that care!" As I've said already, if children are so resilient, how come there are so many adults in therapy trying to make sense of and recover from their childhood?

Question: *Are you creating an oppressive environment for your child/ren or even partner to exist in?*

Action: *If you are, take responsibility for what you are creating and get some help to lift it and create a new environment and energy in which your child/ren or relationship can flourish.*

Meantime, I battled on with the external façade, so as not to be an additional sadness for my mother, and this became the norm as I grew through life. The performance, remember. Many of us do it though, don't we? We have a film over us that is presentable to the outside world, but it is not our authentic being.

My predominant sadness was not feeling Loved in the true sense. Being told I was loved felt empty and served as an additional slap round the face, adding further to the sadness and deepening my pain even more.

I also didn't feel valid, heard or listened to. Hearing and listening are two very different things. We can hear someone speaking, but that doesn't mean to say we are listening to them. I didn't feel heard let alone listened to. The pain of my sadness was so difficult to articulate – it was so deeply rooted.

Being left with others

It often felt like I was left in the care of others who weren't my family, which deep inside of me I hated. My mother had to work to provide for us and has always "had" to work. She chose self-employment, which meant further justification to work, because if she wasn't working she wasn't earning for us and putting food on our table. With my sister suffering many bouts of serious illness during those early years and being hospitalised with pneumonia twice, visits to the doctor's surgery and hospital were quite a regular occurrence. My mother also had a social life. I was taught that was the way in our family unit and so I dutifully got in line with it, but it was so painful and only caused to further impact my already lacking confidence and sense of security.

Having to 'fit in'

I was also the second child, with an easier-going personality, yet I was also of a different mindset to my mother and sister. My sister and mother are out of the same mould and so I was also often described as the "awkward one" because of this. I rarely had a voice because the majority rules, right?

This may give you an idea of how different we are in our preferences, and how tricky it was growing up and living alongside them. My mother and sister enjoyed amateur dramatics and being on stage whereas I preferred doing sport and being outside playing with friends. My sister preferred sailing and I preferred horse-riding. They often seemed to want to be busy, and on the go, distracting their minds with something to do, whereas I am more content going at a slow, calm pace and am happy to sit in peace and contemplation. They are chaotic and often late, while I am organised and generally on time. They don't like confrontation and will display 'ostrich' behaviour, whereas I prefer to get things out on the table and am willing to discuss matters even though it can be painful but so a solution and peace can then reside. They like cultural activities such as the theatre, musicals and the opera whereas I can take or leave them, although I do enjoy traditional ballet. They enjoy reading literature whereas I prefer psychological or spiritual books, and so on.

I'm not saying one set of behaviours is right over the other – they both just are. However, the subtle yet awful underlying nature of being the one who had to 'fit in' ensured I moved further away from authenticity regarding my personality, character and essence. I was not given the space nor opportunity to express my naturalness and I felt more and more overwhelmed by living. I had to exist within the realm of the majority, and slowly my understanding that "I have choice" was quashed and destroyed to the point that I have had to work hard to come to a place where I understand and allow myself to create and choose what I want within my life and what I don't. For a long time, I just went along in life crashing around like a ship with no captain, doing what others wanted of me or what I thought would be acceptable, then if I didn't think it would be deemed acceptable, I'd be secret about it because I'd learned very well how to do that! How crazy, hey?

Chaos and complication

As you can probably gather by now, my mother's thought processes and behaviours can be quite chaotic if not quite toxic too. Many people will say she is kind, and in many ways she absolutely is, but being in her company feels chaotic for my brain and my being. I know I am deeply sensitive – not only energetically, but also in my character so I find it difficult.

Honest, open, kind and fluid communications that only help to provide peace and unity don't exist within my family. It was never encouraged. My mother doesn't know how to communicate other than on a surface level, talking about the weather, what people have done during the day, holiday plans, and so on. On the very rare occasions we have got together to discuss family matters, my mother abstains from the conversation with her usual "I'm listening" comment, or she cries and that's the end of anyone being able to discuss things further, all because she's upset.

My mother doesn't like confrontation, neither does my sister so a space for peace to arise could never been created. They are too resistant to deep peace. Operating in this "let's just ignore it / let's do nothing" manner has meant very little gets discussed and therefore very little gets resolved. Instead tension, frustration, miscommunication, mistakes and non-truths have layered and layered upon each other until they have become mountainous. All on top of such a fragile foundation. It was only ever going to be a matter of time before collapse happened.

So much has been swept under the carpet and not dealt with, honestly and openly too. My mother just desperately wanted to keep things simple by smiling and carrying on as though none of it was happening. Possibly this hooked in to the year she experienced when she was 25, when her dad died, her son died and her husband left to be with another woman. She had to carry on in many ways as she had two young girls to be there for, but years on, by not facing things with reality and being rational about them does not mean things go away. They do not. They just fester until they are like a disease and then it creates havoc.

The crazy thing is, most of what we experienced between us could have been dealt with, sorted and healed had she, in her role as mother, taken responsibility and control of what was happening in the moment. We could have all moved on in much more peace, togetherness and Love. Instead, there is so much complexity and I have found it beyond frustrating and painful, because it hasn't needed to be like this.

Another way my mother's behaviour and actions seem chaotic to me is she's not that conscious about what she's doing. She's muddled and doesn't pay attention to what she's doing. She took us on a trip to France when I was around 13. She couldn't speak French, so my sister managed all of that. I quickly got to grips with the money and the metro map, and she tottered behind letting us lead the way and carry her smiling throughout the four days in a strange foreign city under the guise it was a holiday. That was no holiday for me. For the most part I was internally stressed and frightened, because if anything were to happen to us, my mother wouldn't have had a notion what to do. I was utterly exhausted on the return. Experiences like this have caused me to feel a lot of nervous energy being around my mother. I have often felt on the edge waiting for the next catastrophe, which she would just laugh off or dismiss as me being overly concerned, yet I'd be left picking up the pieces behind her and she didn't realise that either – it's like she operates in total disregard and oblivion.

Often, I lived on the edge of my nerves and for many years I suffered the chaos and the over-complication of life. But not now, it's too exhausting to be around. My mother will never change her ways and why should she in a way – it's her life, right? However, nor is she willing to try to understand what it means to contribute to peace as she is too resistant – just like my sister. They create and act out too much chaos and drama for me to bear. I hold no hate or wish any ill feeling towards them – in fact, it's the opposite. I am able to do this by simply choosing to keep a safe distance from them while allowing the true nature and Integrity of Love to flow as I try to keep an open heart. I don't always succeed, but I continue to try my best.

Being on the end of much jealousy and manipulation

Jealousy is very harmful and if you remember from the outset, anything that is of Integrity in nature doesn't include harmfulness.

My sister was not reined in regarding her jealousy of me as a youngster. I believe this should have been nipped in the bud when we were children – for her sake as well as others and this could have well made a significant contribution and difference to us all having more harmonious, respectful and loving relationships. It was not though, and my understanding is it was because my mother has also been jealous of me so how could she stop her Golden Child from doing a behaviour she was also demonstrating. I could list plenty of examples of her jealousy, but I won't.

Question: *Why be jealous? Why not be happy for the other?*

Question: *What causes such rage that jealousy arises? Look for what is underneath the jealousy, and what is underneath that – what is your deep pain?*

Action: *Leave alone the other person that you are jealous of and work on rooting out your own pain instead.*

Action: *Perhaps you can choose to be joyful for the other person and acknowledge them while celebrating with them and for them whenever an opportunity to do so arises.*

Question: *Do you have children who are jealous of each other?*

Action: *Bring them into respect and happiness for each other with Love.*

Question: *Are you jealous of your partner, sibling, friend or co-worker?*

Action: *Perhaps work on bringing peace to this on your own inside – you will all benefit.*

Separateness

For most of my life I have confused separateness with lack of connectedness. I may not be right, but my belief now is that we are all connected, everything within us and outside of us. There is a matrix, there is a universe, there is energy and there is light, there is consciousness, and we are all connected within that. So being separated from someone doesn't mean we are not connected, because we are.

For example, when someone dear to us passes away, the feelings of separation can be overwhelming for some. However, if we hold in mind that we remain connected on some level, this can perhaps bring in a small degree of peace which can grow as times go by.

I think I struggled with this in the early years of my life, because separation was so harmful for me. I couldn't get near to my mother emotionally (and still can't) nor my father in person or emotionally and obviously this is still the case too.

However, now I realise I can hold the true nature and Integrity of Love in my heart for them as we are all connected, and again that gives a degree of peace.

Lack of confidence

To be 'confident', means 'to rely on'. When we are encouraged to have confidence, we can do that holding Integrity in mind - Wholeness, Honesty, Unity and Non-harmfulness.

What more often happens is that when something is lacking, people are boosted in another area and the gap isn't filled with the confidence needed. This can be why some people who seem overly confident on the outside are more often than not very vulnerable on the inside.

So, for example, I created a monster protection around me for a number of years; the brash 'I can take it all on' type. We all know the type! The one who can be really irritating if you don't allow the true nature and Integrity of Love to flow through you and learn to understand there is a whole being, which includes what lies behind the façade.

Understanding this deeply can be so helpful on many levels and helps to develop an even more generous heart.

Question: *Do you know someone who appears overly confident and arrogant?*

Action: *Contemplate that there is something out of balance within them and next time you interact allow the true nature and Integrity of Love to flow through you, so they too have an opportunity to come into their wholeness.*

Action: *Could you accept them as they are in the moment and allow peace for them, and in turn you.*

Question: *How are you instilling confidence into your child/ren, so they can rely on themselves in wholeness?*

Question: *How are you unearthing your confidence balance within you?*

Lowering self-esteem

With all that goes with abandonment, divorce, bullying, jealousy, control, narcissism, and so on, it's pretty difficult to develop a solid base of esteem and confidence.

Outwardly I may have seemed confident to many. In some ways I was; for one, I was very determined. Inside though, more often than not, I doubted myself. I let others put and pull me down, make me question myself and my capability. I believed more in what I was being told than what my heart was saying on the inside. For instance, my mother would say "You can have anything you want in life", then when I was out there going for it, she'd tug on those invisible strings and I'd quiver in doubt. When I worked in the corporate world, I observed people's jealousy at my ability to get things done and their feelings that I was putting them in a position of weakness. That wasn't my view of them at all – from my heart I was simply doing my job to the best of my ability and getting on with it. I never had intentions of trying to make others feel inferior; this simply wasn't on my radar – I just don't think like that.

Question: *How as a parent are you encouraging and developing your child's esteem and confidence, and do you truly know what it means to do this?*

Question: *How as a sibling have you and are you encouraging your sibling(s) or are you trying to control them?*

Question: *As a boss or manager, how are you creating space for supporting and improving that member of staff who lacks self-esteem (for reasons you will never know and are not your business) but who finds it difficult to progress themselves, perhaps from lack of confidence? Or are you just irritated by them as you don't have the time for this?*

Question: *How as a colleague do you include your fellow colleagues who appear nervous and awkward in company?*

Question: *How as a friend are you not manipulating or trying to control your friend's choices?*

Action: *Be honest with yourself – don't ask yourself and judge yourself. Just simply from your heart ask these questions. Then follow the guidance from your heart centre and ask, "What would the true nature and Integrity of Love do?" You will know, because under all the debris of imprints you are at core Love.*

In your 'Wholeness' you are 'Love'.

Neediness

When a child or adult is needy, they are in pain and there has been a lack of Love in their life along the way. I would put money on that every time. They have been ignored or invalidated or not felt approved of, simply not loved enough and accepted just as they are, in other words in their wholeness.

The best way to overcome neediness is for the person to connect to Love. To be given Love and then shown how they can allow the flow of the true nature and Integrity of Love, i.e. wholeness. Slowly and gently they can come into more peace the more they are able to flow Love and acceptance of the self. It's as simple as that.

Question: *Do you know anyone who is behaving in a needy manner? How can you perhaps help them or encourage them?*

Question: *Can you open your heart and simply accept the being in front of you as they are?*

Action: *Contemplate how it must feel standing in their shoes not to feel whole, not to feel Loved enough, to be lacking.*

Action: *Encourage this person to accept and be kind to themselves too.*

Treading water

As I have said previously, quite often I felt like I was just about coping in the depths of an ocean. Treading water, with my eyes and mouth often dipping below the surface of the water, while my family members were safe and getting on with life on the raft and even sometimes joyfully waving at me obliviously! Clearly this is just how it felt to me and most probably they will have been fighting their own internal battles, but that feeling of constantly being about to go under because the raft wasn't within reach was exhausting.

I sometimes look back and think, why didn't I just swim off in another direction?!

Fear

Often, we get caught up in the vastness of thoughts that are not actually reality – and I'm just as guilty of that when I'm not paying attention and alert to where my mind takes me.

For years I was frightened to walk places in case I was attacked. I was afraid to do things in case my mother would question me in that disapproving manner that put me down to the size she needed to keep me, so I would remain on the end of her strings. The doubt she created and instilled in me caused me to have so much fear. That fear wasn't mine though. I was taking on her thoughts. It took me a long time to realise that and stop reacting to it.

I particularly like Jack Kornfield's way of explaining things as he does so in a beautifully gentle manner. Here he explains how we can overcome our fears…

"Often our fears don't turn out to be accurate predictions of anything. When we become mindful of fearful thoughts, we see the fear is just a story accompanied by dramatic feelings. We don't have to take the story as truth. As we see the productions of our mind, we discover radical freedom. Once we recognise that thoughts are empty, the mind will no longer have the power to deceive us." – Jack Kornfield

Mindfulness training showed me that we don't have to believe our thoughts – they are not fact. When we consider the unhelpful thought of fear, for example, and we ask ourselves "Is that true? Is that really true?!" instead of following the 'story and dramatic feelings', we can really observe the thought of fear and look into it and try to find the 'fear'. I can tell you now, you won't be able to if you really look for it in the moment and you don't get caught up in the 'thought story and dramatic feelings'. We don't need to indulge unhelpful thoughts, but instead we can bring ourselves back to now and simply be with what we find in the moment. We can then turn our mind to more beneficial thoughts for our being, such as "I turn away from that thought of fear and instead drop down into connection through my heart" and reside there a while until I rebalance and then begin again in more peace.

Please be aware though, this is to do with our thoughts. If you feel you are in physical danger, make sure to get yourself safe.

Insecurity

For me the feeling of insecurity mainly links into feeling unsafe and unprotected.

So if you are a parent of young child/ren, thinking you're bored in your marriage and need to spice up your life, or if you choose (notice the word 'choose', not 'need') to leave your child/ren in the care of others on a daily basis while you challenge your mind because bringing up children is often repetitively mind numbing in the early years and difficult as they get older … then think again. Your offspring need YOU. Not a childminder, not another man or woman to be their mum or dad. They need connection to YOU and they will benefit greatly from you being present. Why have children if you do not feel capable or committed to that, because you need to provide them with security for a balanced level of security to be felt, do you not?

Question: *How am I causing my child/ren to feel secure and safe? If you're not, change it.*

Action: *If your child/ren are of an appropriate age, discuss with them how they feel secure and safe. (Just to flag, this discussion never happened in my family, but I can tell you we would have all benefitted if it had happened.)*

Too much identification

When I became aware of this trait, I was a bit surprised to observe I'd been unconsciously playing out this behaviour for the majority of my life. What I mean by too much identification is that I often associated things together in that x means y. So for example, the abuser had a Subaru model car when he was with us. For years after, every time I saw a Subaru car my stomach would turn over and I would be whisked back to the memories of that daily hell on earth I was forced to live in. Years on, my sister bought a Subaru car and I couldn't understand how she didn't make the same connection. Of course, we never discussed it because discussion doesn't happen in our family, remember. But the revulsion I felt having to sit in it that one time was enough.

Identification and association are unhelpful. With mindfulness though, you can prevent this being a problem. It can be a useful tool for those who have suffered mild levels of PTSD or abuse whether mental, physical or emotional. Coming into the present moment of not being in the abusive scenario helps enormously and the flashbacks then can't arise. There can be no identification in the present moment, because you are where you are and that is not back then.

Perfectionism

By not feeling 'enough' to cause my father to stay in our family, and by being on the receiving end of a narcissistic mother, I was always looking over my shoulder as to how I could improve myself and be more and be perfect, because the consequence of not being enough had been devastatingly painful. The unconscious behaviour running was: if I could do something to contribute to being perfect, then I might just be liked or even accepted, loved fully and not abandoned again.

This behaviour also spread out into my corporate career – I never quite felt good enough, always a bit different and awkward and that I must always do better. So I worked my butt into the ground and got burnout twice. My sister also suffered similarly along the way and was off work for a long time while she recovered. You guessed it, it wasn't something that was spoken much about in the family. You see the shame of breaking down meant she was not being perfect and the façade of the great girls my mother was responsible for was in jeopardy, so it was all kept a bit quiet and not shared. We also kept things secret as standard too, of course.

Question: *How can you let go of perfectionist tendencies?*

Question: *Can you realise you are enough just as you are? Perfectly imperfect?*

Action: *Make the decision to accept yourself just as you are right now in the moment, i.e. enough. This can provide more and more peace – practice this.*

Action: *Perhaps consider a phrase to repeat throughout your day, such as "I am enough, just as I am", or "Love flows through me and that is vast".*

The incessant need to fix things/make it okay for others

There are two elements to this for me.

I traced the first back to around age seven. My mother would sometimes fall on to the sofa after dinner exhausted and say, "Will you give my hair a dry shampoo?" To soothe her, I would massage her head and she loved it. I could feel relaxation, relief and peace come into her being as I did this and that made my heart sing. In my heart, I feel this as a positive: "Make it okay for others". This is compassion, namely cherishing others and putting their peace as a priority.

The out of balance element of it though can be traced back to those early years of not making any more pain/difficulty for my parents than they were already having. I also think there is an element of needing to control things when the outer experience is so chaotic or in contrast to what you need for your individual essence, character and personality on the inside. In doing so, I became the one who fixed things or paved the way in preparation for things to be okay or, indeed, swept up afterwards. The supporter or the peace maker so to speak.

One of the most helpful tools I've come across in dealing with this is using the analogy of team sport, for example a netball team, where my role in that team would be to play position of Goal Shooter. In that scenario it is not my responsibility to play Wing Defence. If I try to, I simply foul up. So now when I have the tendency in life to go too much into peacemaker mode for instance, I do my best to bring to mind the team sport. I catch myself and allow others to take responsibility and do their role – it's not my job to do everyone's stuff for them. This realisation has been enormously liberating – it's like a weight lifts and I can relax into being my true essence again. It also offers up the opportunity for others to grow through taking responsibility for their actions, behaviours and decisions.

Growing in the wrong direction

The feeling of "being allowed to be who I am" – a shy, timid and funny girl who just wanted to share in Love, be at peace not at war (whether silent or not) and to rest herself peacefully and in happiness within that – was simply and ironically not permitted.

I was sent to amateur dramatics as a child and teenager. I didn't really enjoy it. I was terrified inside as I stepped on to that stage each night of the performance that I would make a mistake and not be perfect and acceptable, and therefore not loved. Then when it came to being measured for costumes I would be screaming inside with pain. I was a little on the plump side as a child, but of course we just had to get on with it all. My mother thought she was helping me gain confidence by being involved in amateur dramatics; that was her intention for me. But I was constantly forcing myself to go along with it. Going to rehearsals fitted in more with what my mother and sister enjoyed than I did.

I understand my mother was doing her best with the resources she had available and her intention was probably good, but for me and my deep inner needs she was asleep. My father was obviously nowhere to be seen, while my sister was busy being biggest and best. It was really hard being me … the authentic me in my true essence.

Please see your children's inner depth and essence when you are with them – the individuals they are.

So from an early age I began creating a monster shell at times around me to cope and protect that shy, timid light inside. I could be annoying, a bit loud and sometimes showy, but not meaning to be; I was awkward really.

Action: *If there are any annoying/awkward children in your vicinity, contemplate if they may be in pain and how you may be able to help make their pain less rather than amplifying it.*

I wasn't encouraged to be the me who I am. The essence that is me wasn't noticed, cherished and allowed to blossom. I just had to 'fit in' with the busy-ness and chaos of others. I often wonder why didn't my parents choose to look at my essence, nurture and guide that rather than simply doing what they wanted, or giving me what they hadn't had therefore thought I needed in the way that they had wanted it?

This was more often the case in the work place too. Employers didn't seem to encourage development of my intelligence and skills so as to help their businesses flourish nor suggest and support what I could do myself in order to make the most of my potential. I have observed and heard this from so many other people in similar situations too. Appraisal systems and tick boxes, corporate bs, saying one thing and doing another, all in the name of business, stating core values and principles in glossy brochures that are nowhere near the truth of how they operate. Where is the Integrity in that?

Question: *Look around you, are you working in an environment that suits your essence?*

Action: *Takes steps to align with YOUR true core values.*

Action: *If you are in business and have the authority to instigate the implementation of what true Integrity is in your organisation, then have the courage to do it. I implore you to do so, for the sake of all the people who work tirelessly in their Integrity – people are your business, without them there is no business. Guide those who are not coming from a place of Integrity so that they can – and remember that means Wholeness, Unity, Honesty and Non-harmfulness. Hopefully, they will learn the true nature of Integrity, your business will flourish, as will all beings working within it. The vibration of the planet will raise. Now isn't that worth it?*

I was neither encouraged nor guided in the true nature and Integrity of Love. Thank goodness it has been a stronger force than that of the school system, that of the corporate system, that of my family, that of my stubbornness and need to protect myself in the wrong way. When I have followed my intuition and the Integrity flowing inside me, such as when I chose to retrain and become a complementary therapist, I have made really good and wise choices which I have benefitted from, but also those whom I have subsequently come into contact with have too. This is what guides me now.

More abuse and patterns repeating

In adulthood and the realm of intimate relationships, I found myself in further despair. I didn't realise it at the time, but I was choosing to be in relationships with men who enabled me to keep myself in the comfort zone of narcissism, abuse and being left behind for another. I write that now and think how sad. I didn't realise what an unhealthy loop I was in and sabotaging myself so badly.

"Some people will not hear you regardless how much, how loud, how truthful, how loving or how profoundly you speak. Wish them well and let them go." - Anon

It was not all bad though. John was the exception and also a guiding force for me in this area. A hysterically funny and wonderful human being. As he stood by my side, he enabled me to blossom and reconnect with my true essence. From deep within my heart, I am forever grateful.

Confusion and lack of self-esteem within relationships

I was living in the confusion of not being present, not knowing any better, not valuing myself, not raising my game, living life in London in the 90s and socialising loads which meant binge drinking on the weekends. I found myself behaving recklessly, mostly towards myself, but when alcohol was involved and I was on a good time night out with friends, at times I just let caution to the wind and didn't respect myself. Occasionally men took full advantage. It seemed all they wanted to do was paw my body, quite animalistic in a way, but then my body had been pawed since I was age 10, so what was new? At least I guess on such occasions I was giving permission rather than it just happening – or that's how I internalised it.

This is where I believe some men lack responsibility. I see it and hear about it all too often, whereby the man thinks it's the woman's responsibility to set boundaries. I agree it is to a degree, but it is also the responsibility of the men to behave respectfully towards women and implement their knowing and Integrity too – because men know what they're doing and what their motives are, wouldn't you say? That said, I realise some women can be intimidating towards men too. Let Integrity be the guide.

Action: *I ask any man reading this to contemplate, how often have you not taken your responsibility and imposed yourself on a woman? Bearing in mind, you may not know the terrible ordeals she has suffered growing into being a woman – this includes simple verbal remarks too as well as bodily imposition.*

Remember the statistics according to the NSPCC: 1 in 20 children in the UK have been sexually abused and 1 in 3 do not report it for fear of not being believed, or they are threatened and placed in such fear they don't tell, they just suffer because men choose not to control themselves. Ninety percent of sexually abused children are abused by someone they know.

Action: *Parents, you need to teach this to your sons, and stop slapping your teenage sons on the back in a macho, tribal, blooding into manhood type of way. Lads, stop slapping your mates on the back too when they disrespect girls and women. Instead, pull them up on it and ask how that is respectful. Hold open a compassionate heart for all. You will be contributing to creating a better world.*

Abortion

When I was experiencing the "couldn't give a fuck anymore" attitude about myself and why should I when nobody else truly has, I fell pregnant. The short version of the story is that I had an abortion but 'had to' time it right to fall in line with my sister's wedding day.

In my heart I didn't feel capable of being a mother. I mean I could just about look after myself and financially I wasn't in a position to be one either, nor did I have any form of back up or support that I felt I could turn to. It felt like there was no choice other than to have an abortion. I resolved this within myself pretty much straight afterwards. Having an abortion cannot be changed you see. It was a death and so there was no point in wishing it to be different than it was because it never would be. That's not to say I don't occasionally wonder or think about how it might have been, or what age the child might be today and what would their essence be like, but I then choose to get on with my day because these thoughts do not serve me well. As I said, it cannot be changed.

Years after when I shared with my sister what had happened, there was no empathy or compassion, she just told me how awful I was in "God's eyes" and, of course, her eyes too for taking a life. My mother subsequently followed up with "Did you tell your sister that I didn't know either but couldn't have done anything at that time to help you because of being busy with her wedding?" Once again, I fell to my knees in disbelief at my mother's lack of wherewithal and Love. I said to my mother at that point, "I didn't tell you I was pregnant at the time because we don't have that type of relationship". As per usual, my mother remained silent and has never asked me about it since, nor bothered to do anything about the 'state' of our relationship, which I had just pointed out to her. She just carries on obliviously and continues to tell me she loves me, and I continue to think "No, you bloody well don't – you haven't a clue what Love is". We then talk about the weather and what she's up to and then the phone goes down until the next phone call filled with nonsense surface crap. Alternatively, I then go silent because I have no words left. That's the way it is though, and it will probably never change – goodness knows I've done my very best to support her while trying to bring Love in that direction. I then choose to work on forgiveness for her again and again and again, and that is my choice. I remember asking one of my spiritual teachers, "How many times will I have to forgive?" and was told, "As many times as it takes."

Meantime, thank you, Su, for being my friend and confidante at that time; your un-invasive support and allowing the flow of the true nature and Integrity of Love is always in my heart.

Action: *If you have had an abortion and still struggle with having made this decision, for example, maybe you are punishing yourself in some way? Please know you are causing yourself needless suffering. Let yourself off the hook. It cannot be changed, just acknowledged, accepted and learned from. Be kind to yourself and allow yourself to move forward in peacefulness regarding this.*

Burnout twice

Burnout takes a lot to come back from and I only got the message after the second time I experienced it. I busied myself with work, more work and more work, because the work was there to do. I gradually fell into that dreadful hamster wheel of no work-life balance whatsoever. It creeps up on you over time but that phrase "I'll just do this and then I'll be done" has since been deleted from my being. Before I knew it, I regularly put in a 12-hour day plus I worked at the weekends for extended periods of time. At the time I felt I had to because the work demands were there and if I didn't deliver, well … I couldn't contemplate the consequences. It was intensely pressurised and on many different levels. The knock-on effects included: not feeding myself properly with nourishing food because there simply wasn't time to shop, cook, run a home, and so on, as well as work. My social life became non-existent too. I wasn't really paying attention to anything other than the To Do List that had become my life, which essentially was built on fear. It was horrendous, but these days all of this seems to have become 'normalised' for so many people. I see and hear about it in my complementary therapy practice all too often. That doesn't make it okay though and employers have a responsibility not to allow it, let alone expect that of individuals. What employers are also doing by not taking responsibility and instead creating intense pressure on their employees with unsustainable workloads also has a knock-on effect for the likes of the NHS. Too many people are turning up in their doctors' surgeries with work-related stress. This wouldn't be necessary if employers and their management teams were coming from a place of Integrity; surely employers have a duty not to be causing such a drain on NHS resources, don't they? Also, employees must be able to implement their boundaries and adhere to their contractual hours without feeling the fear of losing their job, which again I often hear from people.

Things need to change as people cannot sustain this. It's also a false economy for the companies. According to the Health and Safety Executive government website, which cites the Labour Force Survey, 15.4 million working days were lost in the UK due to work-related stress, depression or anxiety during 2017/18. That is a massive cost to people and their lives but also the economy.

My belief is that I also suffered adrenal fatigue during this time. The amount of cortisol pumping round my body must have been very high because the weight I put on in such a short space of time was abnormal. Add to that the amount of adrenaline circulating at an all-time high because of the intense pressure I was working under – I was heading for disaster and this was the last straw. When I looked back, I had probably been operating on high alert since my early childhood, in fact from the moment of hearing yelling and screaming when I was two or three years old. And then my body said, "Enough is enough". For me, this phase of extreme pressure was the straw that broke the camel's back and my body shut down.

As I have come to understand it, many of the symptoms of adrenal fatigue are similar to that of depression, but adrenal fatigue does not seem to be recognised by western medicine. There is a great book about this called *Adrenal Fatigue – the 21st Century Stress Syndrome*. It's by James L. Wilson and I'd really recommend it for anyone suffering and heading for burnout.

Of course, when I visited my doctor, they asked what now seems to be a standard question: "Would you like some anti-depressants?" NO, FLIPPING NO! I just needed some time out of the horrendousness that was the work environment in order that I could catch my breath, recover and reset, but I did not realise how empty of resource I had been brought to during this period.

Symptoms following burnout include loss of ability to memorise things as before. It's like the neural pathways have been so overloaded they really do get burned so they can't function. Extreme exhaustion. Inability to hold back the tears. PTSD symptoms, for example at the thought of going back into the environment. Lack of confidence and self-belief. Self-loathing. Anxiousness and panic. Loss of libido. Despair. The inability to cope with any pressure or stress. The need for quiet and stillness. Feelings of numbness and so on. It's not pretty. I remember not being able to get out of bed until 4pm one afternoon shortly after I'd been signed off by my doctor with work-related stress.

On the road to recovery, I remember saying to myself, "If I can do two things today, that will be enough and one of those things will be walking my dog, Evie." That meant the other might have been to wash up, or vacuum, or do some grocery shopping. Then I'd have to rest. I couldn't physically or mentally cope with doing any more than that.

I'd say it took my bodymind a good nine months to recover from the effects of that burnout.

Question: *How is your work/life balance?*

Question: *Are you eating healthy fresh food and drinking lots of water?*

Question: *Do you take a lunch break at work and get outside into fresh air or away from your work place?*

Question: *Do you have time out in your day if you are a full-time parent or carer to sit and be present and do nothing but that?*

Question: *Are you drinking alcohol or taking recreational drugs to bring your stress levels down?*

Question: *Are you aware of your breath and connecting with the rhythm of your breath and your body at any point in the day?*

Action: *See if you can hold your attention on your breath for 5 seconds and not think of anything else – if you can't then you may find it helpful to make some changes.*

Brokenness

I broke open when I hit burnout for the second time – I didn't get the message the first time. I bounced back much more easily the first time too. Again, not being present and awake was ruling the day instead at this point, I simply had to get the job done and the pressure was very much on me in various ways including to deliver, deliver, deliver.

I had peaked in my pain and I crumbled. My body could no longer hold me in place the way my mind was operating, and nor should it have had to. Nor could it cope with the amount of cortisol and adrenaline pumping round it.

I had got so far away from my natural nature and essence and I hadn't realised it – AGAIN! So my ever kind body informed me the best way it could and it broke. I was lifeless, limp, barely able to function.

Today I can congruently say, I'm glad I broke open. It enabled me to reveal and reconnect to my authentic beingness, you see, and in that the ability to breathe in life more easily. It also enabled my essence to be the shy, quiet, kind being who also possessed some humour, bluntness and innate feisty drive for fairness, and compassion for all. One who holds dearly the wish that Integrity can be the order of the day if enough of us make the effort for it to be so. For as long as I can remember, I have understood – with almost an innate knowing – that every being has a light inside them, and that light can shine brightly given the opportunity and supported by a willingness not to deviate from it.

"Sometimes when we think our life is falling apart, what we don't see is that it might just be falling into place." - Anon

Aloneness

It often felt as though I was alone in my life because nobody else experiences life through the same eyeballs and heart as we do ourselves. I haven't felt lonely though, because I'm content in my own company and I have been fortunate to have wonderful friends in my life too, but I've felt alone in the sense of not having a loving family connection or back up from them or a loving partner. That's a very dark place at times, but again, so many people understand this feeling and suffer it as well as the consequences of feeling it, I don't doubt.

We may isolate ourselves, we may go into depression, we may feel as though we're in an ocean of despair, but we can lift ourselves by going inwards to begin with. Coming to accept what is there and being peaceful with what we find. The more we sit in stillness with ourselves and all that arises there, the more the darkness can dissipate.

I'm not sure where I came across this saying, but I acknowledge and thank them right here, right now. May it give you hope too and be a nudge along your path if you are currently feeling in a dark place.

"It is only when we are truly alone, without someone else to lean on, left with our own inner solitude, that we can undergo a process of change. The introspection that is needed to bring out the light that has dwindled down to ash and reignite the fire of our being. So let the darkness shape you, let it reform you, let it cradle you and birth you into a new life. Let the spark flame again, in the darkness is where you will find it." - Anon

Please also know there is much more going on in the universe and the vastness of it than we can ever possibly understand as humans. We are connected to so much beauty and exquisiteness if we allow ourselves to open to it.

Suicidal thoughts

There are a number of times in my life the thought of ending my life passed through my mind as a result of mental and emotional overwhelm. I could never have carried through with it, but I remember driving down the road one day and being low enough to think, "This is so painful I just want to die, and it would be so easy to let my car drive into that tree".

It's a very dark place to be, but I want anyone out there reading this to know that it is possible to come out of that darkness. Only you can do it, but support is there so do seek help if you need.

Action: *Perhaps take yourself to a group environment where you can talk about your pain if you want to, or you can learn to sit with what you find such as in a meditation or prayer group.*

Action: *Perhaps seek help on a one-to-one basis – maybe call the Samaritans or talk to your doctor, a therapist or friend.*

Know you are acceptable just as you are though in this moment. Know the Integrity of Love is there just waiting for you to allow it to flow through you so as to connect fully within you. Know you can meld with Love, you are Love, be Love.

Struggle

For much of my life, it has been a struggle financially but mainly I was just surviving mentally and emotionally within the oppressive dynamic that is my family. To date, though, I have not struggled physically or spiritually. That is a blessing for me for which I am humbly grateful. However, as Adam taught me at a young age, illness and death are coming to us all and it doesn't discriminate – I do acknowledge this.

There are people who struggle in different ways though. Some have horrendously difficult physical struggles, or care for others that do. Yet they may not struggle so much financially. This is why understanding Dharma teachings about karma has been so helpful for me personally as it helps reduce the want and need to blame others for our personal struggle and suffering. I am living a human life and I am responsible for the causes and conditions arising in this lifetime, because of my previous thoughts and actions in this and past lifetimes. If I am to struggle and suffer less in the future as well as in future lifetimes, then it is in the present moment that I must create those causes. So my deep wish and what I strive for in this lifetime is to be compassionate to all beings, share kindness, be supportive, and help others out of pain. My overarching wish is for others not to have to struggle or be in pain, for the true nature and Integrity of Love to be present in our hearts and minds. I came in with that nature – that is my essence – I know this deeply – it is a knowing. I can't explain it in any other way. However, that is why I choose to openly share my story, to help others shorten the pain they may experience and in turn heal more quickly if they can.

Blame

For years I blamed my circumstances and family for my pains. They are accountable for their behaviour and actions, but I don't blame them anymore. Let me tell you, the path of blame doesn't take us anywhere positive. We give ourselves away to the other when we blame. We place ourselves in the position of victim and being the effect.

When we step to the other side and place ourselves in the position of cause rather than effect, we then have more options and control to create the life we want. Don't waste a moment longer blaming others – it's fruitless. If you are not letting them off the hook for their crimes either, you just end up staying on the hook underneath them until you let go of it all. Or if the image of a tug of war represents this better, simply put down your end of the rope and wish the others well. Then move on in your life, however you choose to do that.

Question: *Who and what is pressing your buttons?*

There are two beneficial things you can do when you are irritated by someone or something – and they don't include getting angry on the inside and smiling on the outside! Instead you can refrain from blaming the other. Then you can turn inwards and ask yourself: "Why am I irritated, what is this trying to show me about what I can heal or needs healing?" Then work on that and take appropriate action.

The other person is as they are, you are the one irritated, you are the one having the reaction. Someone else may not have that reaction when they see the other, instead they might have butterflies in their stomach. I repeat, you are the one having the irritation (which can be termed a form of anger) and therefore you have something to work on.

This is a really powerful way to come more into peace and calmness. It can also help you take responsibility for where your mind is taking you, while coming more into acceptance of others.

Guilt and remorse

There are things I've done in my life I have felt guilty and remorseful for. This is mainly for my actions and behaviours done to others.

However, there is a positive that comes from acknowledging your own guilt and that is you take back responsibility – in doing so you can change your behaviour and actions going forward.

I have therefore come to understand and learned how to hand back the shame that does not belong to me and while I still find it difficult (because I still don't like others being in pain), I know that it is not my responsibility to carry the consequences for other people's behaviours and actions, simply because they don't want to own their own shit, nor be willing to come from a place of Integrity.

Where we have guilt and remorse, we can take responsibility for it and look to make peace there.

This is why understanding the difference between shame as opposed to guilt/remorse has been so liberating. Off-loading the shame to the ground allows so much more room for the Integrity of Love to flow – and it's so beautiful when it does.

Shame

Shame is often referred to as painful feelings about how we appear to others or ourselves but doesn't necessarily depend on us having done anything. On top of all the pain I was experiencing, I was groomed by a narcissist and this is why I found healing shame to be even more difficult. My mother has never outwardly owned and acknowledged her actions – to this day she defends herself and doesn't budge in her behaviour. I can sort of smile about it now, but it can also still be painful on occasion too.

Shame has been my Achilles heel and what needed most healing. I didn't realise it, but shame was almost part of my DNA and it didn't reveal itself fully for healing until I'd done a lot of other inner healing and after being fully cracked open. Underneath all the crap I was dealing with from my childhood and gently cleansing, there were layers and layers of shame – the list was endless! Here are some from the list:

Shame of being from a divorced, damaged and broken family

Shame of being abandoned

Shame of being poor

Shame of not being an academic like my sister

Shame of being the awkward one

Shame of being sexually abused

Shame of being so controlled by a narcissist

Shame of my body

Shame of being innately shy

Shame of lacking confidence

Shame of lacking so much

Shame of not being enough

Shame of not being loved nor feeling lovable

…and so on…

Throughout the years I know people have thought I was depressed. In my heart I know this has not been the case. I have been overwhelmed by carrying the load described in this book and not being able to help my family turn to see the true nature and Integrity of Love. I've often been despairing of it, but not depressed. There is a difference.

Frustratingly gobsmacked, hugely angry and despairing that they did not acknowledge my pain, but instead they waved from the raft or turned to socialise or live their life not giving a damn. Yes – I have been that too, but not depressed.

So many people are offered or put on medication these days and as I said, I've been offered it in the past too. In my view there is generally only one winner where anti-depressants are concerned and ultimately that is the pharmaceutical companies. These drugs seem to help numb and help people block out the pain. They don't necessarily heal it. They don't get to the root of the suffering, they don't provide true peace, they are a temporary numbing facilitator – this is just my view. Yet what if we all just opened our hearts a bit more to each other, considered others more equally and wholly and asked them "What is your pain?" then hung around to help them. Surely, there would be less need for so many pharmaceutical companies which profit hugely, cause heinous cruelty to animals along the way and zombify humans. I realise that is judgemental on my part, but I wholeheartedly stand firm in this, because I don't believe they help people heal their inner pain and suffering at core.

A friend of mine who is very awake on many levels described a time when her son reached teenagerhood. Hormones began racing around his system, mood swings were the norm, his behaviours changed totally, rows and strops happened daily and gone was that sweet, cute little boy that had been there just days before.

She then relayed the moment she and her husband discussed the pain he must be experiencing. They created a space as a family and asked him what his pain was. Their teenage son raged at this too saying how they knew nothing and to stop being so stupid – they just didn't get it! However, they took the time and persisted in holding the space of loving kindness while asking the question, "What is your pain?" They created a space for open honesty and in a short space of time, communication about the pain began to surface and healing was enabled. The true nature and Integrity of Love flowed.

As a child, all I needed was space to be created from time to time and to be asked, "What is your pain and what do you need?" For my pain to be heard, listened to, acknowledged and acted upon appropriately. For my feelings to be acknowledged and not swept away with invalidation and a sweeping statement such as "Don't be silly, it's not like that".

It's not rocket science this stuff. We just need to SLOW DOWN and connect to the compassion in our hearts where others are concerned as well as ourselves. We need to be willing to put others before ourselves too on occasion. We need to stop the world of 'me and I' and we need to be deeply willing and committed to allowing in the true nature and Integrity of Love to our lives. Wholeness, Honesty, Unity and Non-harmfulness.

By letting go of shame, we can then come from a place of Integrity and in doing so we create wholeness in all that we do. Can you imagine if all humans came from a place of Integrity how wonderful that would be? Only we can create that though. So may I invite you in your daily activities to come from Integrity and let that ripple outwards into the world. Let us GIVE that to this beautiful planet we have the privilege of sharing in each and every day it gives us life. Let us stop taking so much from the planet and let us GIVE more to her in the way that she needs, not the way we want to give to her without care and kindness for her needs, but what is beneficial and good for her. Let us open our hearts and really listen to earth's pain. Let us connect deeply with her and listen to and hear what it is she is silently crying out for – she will whisper it to us. Let us support her out of her pain. Let us also listen to each other from the space of Integrity.

"I alone cannot change the world, but I can cast a stone across the waters to create many ripples" – Mother Teresa

Lack of trust

Over the years I placed too much trust in others, I put blind faith in others with their own agenda, or their need to control, manipulate and often lacking Integrity. It clearly turned out not to be for my benefit, so even to this day it takes quite a lot for me to trust others. I read recently that this can indicate a need for protection still, and only when we don't feel the need for protection, are we truly free.

My instincts have always been there – just like yours are for you. However, when we are so taken away from our authentic self, we lose our ability to connect to, listen to and act upon what our intuition proves to us.

These days I know to trust in me and my intuition again, trust in energy, trust in the true nature and Integrity of Love. Reiki began this reconnection for me and it has taken me on a deeply healing journey for which I don't have words vast enough to share my gratitude, so instead I just stay connected and I'm learning more and more to trust in life itself.

Trust your intuition – it will be right. However, if you don't feel aligned to it then seek out some help to reconnect to it. If you're unsure, simply ask yourself, "What would the true nature and Integrity of Love do?" and let this guide you.

Part 5:
Healing the Pain

So how did I begin to heal this little lot, and why should I have had to? I've often asked myself why I should have experienced all this struggle, suffering and pain which wasn't necessary in the first place had there been a bit more awareness and Love present. I have been alone and bereft within my family and angry for years because how could they not see that it's our actions causing it, and all that was needed was true Love to be present and flowing in all of us. I just didn't get it, until these last few years I guess. Learning about karma has helped me enormously with this; in other words, the actions I have created in the past including past lives have caused the results I experience in this lifetime. Many of my healing teachers and supporters have said to me along the way, you are gifted at what you do, how you help others out of pain and heal along their journeys. Being the shy, timid type I couldn't quite take this to heart; it was a compliment, after all, and they can be challenging for me to receive. However, perhaps I could not help people without having had the experience of so much pain and learning how to heal through it. Perhaps that also means I can contribute to helping raise the vibration of the true nature and Integrity of Love on this planet through this book.....we'll see.

The healing journey began in earnest the moment I had my first Reiki treatment back in 1999, and I soon learned how once you step on the path of healing there is no going back! I have deviated a bit at times, but soon found my way back. I have been fortunate with having such dear and special friends whose Love and support has been so wholesome. My journey has also encompassed:

- Gifted and supportive teachers
- Healing energies;
    - Reiki
    - Neuro-Linguistic Programming
    - Clinical massage
    - The bodymind connection
    - Homeopathy
    - Presence – mindfulness and meditation
    - Bach Flower Remedies

- Courage
- Change
- Honesty
- Slowing down
- Learning
- Determination
- Recovery from narcissism
- Recovery from child sex abuse
- Healing anger
- Boundaries
- Shining true light
- Queen Evie
- Responsibility
- Apologising sincerely
- Non-judgementalness
- Acceptance and resistance
- Self-care
- Equalness
- Essence and spirit
- Understanding my mind
- The past is the past
- Authenticity
- Questioning Integrity
- Understanding it's an inside job
- … a continuing journey …

In 1985 after that night of Live Aid, when the abuse was revealed, my mother found me a counsellor, but I refused to go back after the first session. At that time it caused me more damage in that one session than I needed. The lady asked me to relay why I was there, so I told her everything about the abuse culminating in the night of Live Aid, dutifully doing what was asked of me – that's what can happen being the daughter of a narcissistic mother who was strict and the child under the watch of a sexually abusive alcoholic – you do as you're told.

At the end of my download to her, it felt like such a relief as I thought I was finally being heard, listened to and believed. I thought I would receive the help I so desperately needed, and action would be taken finally. Instead, she sat there with her hands crossed in her lap and said, "Very good, come back next week". It was if I'd just been hung by a rope around my neck and left to dangle for my life, just hanging in mid-air. WHAT?! NO HELP IN THAT MOMENT AT ALL – AGAIN!!! I was further deeply traumatised. The pain and anger soared from throughout my whole body and my head spun in bitter confusion. I refused to go back to her. How could anyone not give any reassurance that this hell I'd been living in was not normal but was now over, while assuring me that man would not be allowed near me again. How could I not be told that I was now safe, that things would get better and these sessions would help and how? The healing journey went on pause and school continued; I had to study and had school exams to prepare for after all. Yes – all of this was going on around a most crucial time of my school life.

A year or so later I found myself really struggling with zero confidence. I took my healing into my own hands this time and it's one of the best things I've ever done. I came across Neuro-Linguistic Programming (NLP), which was fairly new to the UK back then in 1987 and had a couple of sessions in order to help me gain at least a couple of degrees of confidence. It certainly helped and that sowed a seed for later when I was living in London.

It is tough writing this even now, with all my knowledge and experience. PTSD is often difficult to manage as the slightest thing can fling you back into the memories and emotions of the darkness, so it takes a lot of discipline to remain detached while I share this with you. However, I pause, I sit, I breathe, I come back into the present and I allow the true nature and Integrity of Love to flow through me, so I can continue in ease.

Wonderfully supportive friendships

Oh, where would I be without them all?! My heart swells with Love and gratitude when I think of their kindness, their compassion, the hours and experiences we have shared and the amount of Love they have flowed to me.

To give you an idea, when I told one friend about some of my experiences I've described, he said, "I can hear and feel your pain". My whole body relaxed in that moment. Not one member of my own family has ever said anything like that over the years. Like many of my friends, he noticed it and he opened the conversation about it – he didn't shy away, he didn't say "Well, this has happened to me," making what I had just told him irrelevant. He didn't defend any of my family in that moment. He could stand in my shoes and then be supportive. That is true empathy.

I have been so fortunate along my path to have so many people in my life that I can call true friends, some of whom are mentioned at the start of this book. It's not possible to mention them all here, but they know who they are and they know the wonderfully loving and caring friendships we have between us – each one very different and each one very dear to me.

I think one of the best gifts you can give anyone and also receive is true listening and non-judgementalness. Many of my friends have listened and heard me and I hope I do the same for them. The ability to be our true selves is so valuable too – shitty one day and okay the next, supportive one day and not able to be the next. For me, our friendships are rooted in deep respect, true acceptance and the true nature and Integrity of Love flows through them.

Gifted and supportive teachers

Stewart Ivory taught me Reiki. He was so down to earth, gentle, kind, respectful with a mischievous edge. Being in his company was probably the first time I'd felt safe in the company of a man. I was 29.

Reiki put me properly on the path to recovery. In my humble opinion, it's a powerful, intelligent, loving, light energy that deserves utter respect from us as humans. It is beyond our human comprehension as far as I'm concerned, and that's what I impart when teaching the four levels of training. This is where I first came across Integrity in more depth. We were taught to use our intuition, intent and integrity. Then to trust it, let it do its stuff and be guided by it; this way we wouldn't go wrong, and I have shared this in my teachings too. As practitioners of it, we are mere conduits – it is not us doing the healing, it is Reiki doing it, and I never forget that.

I studied NLP with Hans and Jeremy – they taught me loads about how we operate as humans, such as coping strategies and how we communicate with ourselves and others. My willingness to question perceptively has a lot to do with my training with these guys.

Meg and Rachel of Jing Advanced Massage helped expand my knowledge and understanding of massage therapy treatments. They encouraged me, nurtured me and gave me revolutionary tools and techniques which gave me confidence in my clinical massage work. For many years this proved to be the foundation of my career in complementary therapies. This field of work is where I have been most comfortable, confident in and good at – I can say that now, even if it has taken quite a while for me to acknowledge myself enough to say it!

Gayle, Judith and Paula introduced me to mindfulness. In 1999, I read a book called *The Power of Now* by Eckhart Tolle and afterwards heard him speak at a seminar in London, where Annie Lennox was sitting behind me. I didn't quite know which way to look first as I sat in awe of them both! Anyway, years later this book came into its own again for me when I read it for the second time during my mindfulness teacher training.

At the Kadampa Meditation Centres (KMC), I learnt more about meditation and Dharma teachings. As an eight-year-old, I went on a school trip to Manjushri Kadampa Meditation Centre. It was 20 minutes' drive from our school in Cumbria, and I was instantly transfixed and fascinated by every bit of it. My mother took me there too for a visit around the same time. However, it was a bit too "whacky" for her and I was discouraged from exploring such things as Buddhism as, in her words, "They're just dropping out of society – you can't get away from yourself that easy." If only she had explored it herself, she would have come to understand it's so much more, including how it isn't necessary to make such incorrect judgements. Anyway – I dipped into it again in my 30s and it was also beneficial then. Training in mindfulness reignited my interest in meditation a few years later, and after that I spent many hours at classes in the temple taking in more of Buddha's teachings. Studying in this way further helped me to tame my mind.

I find so much wisdom and beauty in Buddha's teachings but there is still so much for me to learn and grow within it; there are after all 84,000 teachings and then so much more within all of that. So I hold the wish that the conditions will arise for me in due course. This community offers many things including gentleness, loving kindness, happiness and, of course, exquisite wisdom through the teachings. When I first started visiting KMC on a more regular basis it was like each time I went, there was an invisible hand there to hold the chair in place while I sat down in relief and moved more into peace with each sitting and slowly my mind was able to come more into peace. Don't get me wrong, it can be challenging too, of course, as the mind and ego are questioned, but that feeling of relief is always so welcome.

Healing energies

I feel so privileged to know the 'guides', for want of a better word, who have entered my life and to have experienced their many wisdoms and talents. I properly stepped onto the healing path when I came across Reiki in 1999 and it's been one heck of a journey – one I surely wouldn't have missed.

Reiki

For those not familiar with Reiki, it is a form of energy healing. All living beings have energy running through them and sometimes this can be out of balance and so, for example, the human being operates at a lower level vibration than is effective. During the Reiki treatment, the client by being there invites the energy to them, while the practitioner places their hands on the fully clothed body, primarily at the chakra points, acting as a conduit for the energy to flow through them for the benefit of the recipient. They channel the Reiki energy which, as I mentioned earlier, is an intelligent high vibrational energy beyond human comprehension – it is aligned to the vibration of Love. We may try to understand it with our brains, but we can't fully. It flows through the practitioner into the recipient for their balance, highest good and greatest joy. The recipient's energy system is flooded with Reiki's higher vibration and then encouraged to come more into alignment with that higher vibration. Anything that is of a lower vibration (such as depression or anxiety) cannot exist in its current form and has to raise its game or dissipate, which may for instance be in the form of tears.

I went for treatments and my world changed during the first six treatments I had. I cried a lot and in so doing I allowed my being to release and the healing journey accelerated. I was blown away by the positive impact Reiki had on me. I felt stronger, more stable and balanced, more able to move ahead in a more positive manner than I'd felt in a long time. We are energetic systems, so why would we not treat our energy?

During one of the treatments I experienced a lot of metaphysical stuff and the practitioner suggested I look into training in Reiki myself. The first level of training involves learning to treat the self. This was wonderful – I now had instant access to healing myself! It shone light into my life when I was in a place of such deep darkness. I experienced much benefit and I wanted to share this incredible energy with others. Over time I trained in all of the four levels incorporated in the formalised training. I taught Reiki for many years and I have never ceased to be deeply moved by the levels of shift into peace people can gain from it. To this day I still treat myself with Reiki, while also providing treatments for others in my complementary therapy practice.

Once I connected with Reiki, things began to change and although the healing journey has been gruelling in parts, once I stepped onto that path there was no turning back. Much of my sadness lifted, but there was still something at my core that wasn't shifting. That said, I was in a far better place inside than I'd been in my family life so for the time being I'd take that in spades!

Neuro-Linguistic Programming (NLP)

In 1999 I also began training in NLP. One of its main pillars is understanding the way we communicate with ourselves and others, including strategies and patterns we operate. NLP had been helpful when I was 17 following my escape from the abuse, and for some reason it popped up on my radar again – there are no co-incidences. I was beginning to trust my intuition more and let myself be led by that.

So there I was, working in an advertising agency in London during the day while in the evenings and at weekends training in Reiki and NLP. Reiki was pretty much unheard of back then and so deemed totally whacky and tree-huggy and I soon became known as "the white witch". NLP was a buzz word and loads of people were getting on the bandwagon. It's quite a bit more left brained than Reiki so I was definitely using both sides of my brain during that time, let's just put it that way.

What NLP gave me in the long term was an understanding of my thinking self and an ability to ask really perceptive questions, and if you can ask great questions then you can hope to achieve great answers. This was really helpful with digging through the layers and layers of crap I'd built up over the years. It was extremely useful training and I incorporate some of the techniques into my complementary therapy practice too of course, for the benefit of others.

If you remember at the outset, I mentioned my earliest memory was my parents yelling and screaming at each other. This was my foundation, and during my NLP training I realised how fundamental it is to have secure and balanced foundation in those early years of life, the first seven being the most important. Well – you've read what my first few years involved, and they were nothing close to secure or balanced. They were fraught with chaos, fear and insecurity and that just got layered and layered and layered upon until 1999, when I finally began to gently peel them back.

I often liken this process to carefully assisting the petals of a peony to unfold. The petals are so delicate and need gentle care if they are not to be ripped and harmed in the process. However, what opens when the flower blossoms is utter joyous beauty and so worth being patient for. Life is life, and we are here to unfold and blossom, are we not?

Clinical massage

During my Reiki training I came across the concept 'What goes on in the mind can manifest in the body'. This soon became one of the pillars of my complementary therapy practice, particularly as I began to understand how much of what goes on in our mind can get stored in our body and show us where our mind is at. I'll talk more of this later in the section on Bodymind.

This connection was fascinating for me and I was like a sponge for it. I decided to train in massage, initially to further my Reiki practice. I thought if I understood more about the anatomy and physiology of the human being, maybe I could understand in more depth the bodymind connection.

I did a lot of advanced training with Jing Advanced Massage Training including myofascial release. I was in my element and was so motivated to learn more and more about how utterly phenomenal the human body is. I found Rachel and Meg at the conception of their training school, but I could see they were revolutionaries – in fact, that was one of their tag lines: "Let's start a revolution", and my goodness they did!

One of their primary goals was to share their knowledge openly and in a succinct way, so all those therapists who came through their school would not have to go through everything the founders did in finding the quickest and most effective methods for treating the body. That is Integrity, and I felt it from the off. That is true giving, and I felt that from the off too. Great knowledge, great sharing, great energy awareness. Bingo! I'd found beings who were allowing the true nature and Integrity of Love to flow through them for the benefit of others.

Meg and Rachel taught me (and of course many others) massage techniques that gave me confidence in my natural abilities to help people out of pain. They helped raise my self-esteem and to begin to know my worth as a person as well as a therapist. I built a very successful complementary therapy practice which I ran for 10 years and absolutely loved it. I then had some time out for a couple of years but returned to it again in 2015.

The bodymind connection

Awareness of the bodymind connection is fundamental in my therapy practice. I see it all too often, day in, day out, for it not to be brought to light: what goes on in the mind can manifest in the body. Reading Debbie Shapiro's book, *The Bodymind Workbook* was pivotal for me back in 2002. She also wrote *Your Body Speaks Your Mind*, which is just as useful.

She explains many aspects of how the mind and body work together, from the left and right brain's influence over the opposite sides of the body, to the functionality of organs in relation to the mind, to limbs, and how our emotions and thoughts can affect and become stored in the human being system.

As an example, here is an excerpt from her book where she describes how the liver can be functioning in correlation with the mind and in turn affects our day-to-day living experience:

> "The liver deals with excess fats, proteins and sugars, helping to extract them from the blood and then to eliminate them. It is literally our life-giver. It is also known as the seat of anger, a place where anger is stored, for keeping the blood clean can mean having to extract the negativity from it. It is intimately connected to addictive behaviour and especially to the repressed anger of which addictive behaviour can be a manifestation. Liver disorders often give rise to depression, which can be seen as anger turned towards ourselves. Liver sluggishness affects spiritual and inner levels of awareness; then we lose purpose and direction. For the liver gives us life, just as it can harbour our fear of life."

I truly believe when we heal the pain in our mind, our body can rest in relief and peace.

It can therefore help to realise how utterly astounding we humans are. If you haven't seen the Body Worlds exhibition, I'd encourage you to do so if you get the opportunity – it really shows in astonishing detail and overwhelmingly what we take for granted as the human body.

As an example, it takes 34 muscles to move the 29 bones in the hand and fingers. Both my hands are moving right now as I type out the pages of this book. Simultaneously my heart is beating and pumping blood round my body, my lungs are breathing in oxygen and breathing out CO_2, my eyes can see, I can smell, hear and taste the tea I occasionally sip as I type with the other hand. My kidneys are working, my nervous system is constantly sending signals, my brain is doing its thing, hormones are being monitored and sent, my gut is processing my lunch, my hair is growing, as are my nails, my feet are connecting me to the earth, my thoughts are running, my emotions are peaceful, my energetic system is at work, and so the list goes on and on and on. Yet we don't seem to appreciate the intricacies and wondrousness that our bodies are.

Question: *Have you ever noticed how phenomenal your bodymind really is?*

Action: *Contemplate this for a moment and relate it to your own being.*

Question: *Going forward, what can you do each day to show your bodymind appreciation?*

Action: *Look at your hands for a couple of minutes and contemplate what they have done for you just today.*

Action: *Take your attention to your breath as you breathe in and out for a few moments. Now realise in this moment, your body has been breathing for you day and night since the moment you were born. Your body has done this for you unconditionally, you haven't had to ask it to do this for you in each moment day and night – it simply does it. Appreciate that every day from now on.*

Action: *Sit with your body for 10 minutes each day observing it, noticing the phenomenal thing that houses your spirit and mind, or even as you're walking or running, if you're fortunate to be able to do this.*

Action: *Give thanks to it.*

All too often we berate our body for being too fat or too thin, our hair for being too curly or straight. We are not always conscious how we are nourishing our body or what a battering we are giving it. We may work out at the gym during the week and go on a socialising food and drink binge at the weekend, then repeat the next week. They give us messages about where our minds are and yet we ignore them until in desperation they break or fracture. Then for a short time we realise how we take our bodies for granted. That is until we are recovered and crack on doing it all over again.

Action: *Each day, change the messaging you give to your body. Instead of saying I hate my hair, perhaps say I'm grateful that my hair grows.*

Action: *Some people's hair isn't growing right now – for example due to chemo/radiotherapy. Take a few moments to contemplate that and how that might be, while noticing how ungrateful you have been simply because you may have curly hair instead of straight hair.*

Homeopathy

I have never trained in homeopathy, but I do use it for medicinal purposes. Western medicines are too harsh on my system. I remember convulsing and fainting when I had a jab before going on a holiday and that for me was enough to make me think there must be another way.

During yet another phase of being suppressed by others, not feeling like I had a voice, not feeling listened to or heard, being invalidated, my body suddenly showed me the symptoms known in western medical terms as acute thyroiditis. I knew from my massage training that any medical term ending 'itis' is inflammation, so I wasn't surprised as I was raging inside at the disbelief of those around me and their lack of foresight and logic. Neither was it a surprise to me that my body reacted so violently as it was a tipping point for me regarding not being heard or listened to.

My throat and neck swelled to the point my chin was indefinable. I was having night sweats, waking up dripping wet. I lost a stone in weight in just over a week. I had no energy yet my mind was racing, I was overly anxious and like a paranoid lunatic because I was on such high alert. I could barely eat because my throat had swollen so much, except I was craving egg sandwiches. Eggs are a good source of iodine, and interestingly my thyroid was telling my brain what it needed. My doctor diagnosed acute thyroiditis and I was booked in to see a consultant. Meantime I had some craniosacral therapy immediately and that helped reduce the swelling in my neck. The craniosacral therapist then passed me on to Vinciane Ollington, a wonderful homeopath. Vinciane had been told by her doctor years earlier that she would need to have her diseased thyroid removed. This gland is one of the most important in our body and fundamental to our functionality. This news prompted her to learn more about homeopathy and so much so she became qualified. Incidentally, she did not have her thyroid gland out and she still has it 20 years on. I was in good and confident hands. Vinciane prescribed the relevant pills and within the year all my thyroid levels were back to normal when tested. The consultant had wanted to put me on thyroxin for the rest of my life. There was no way I was going to contemplate such a notion – why would I when there were other more natural and less invasive options available? As far as I was and still am concerned, it was a bodymind matter. Heal the mind, you heal the body. That is my view and I appreciate not how everyone will choose to view it.

Western medicine absolutely has its place of course – I certainly don't deny that. There are many many talented people working in that field and performing miracles every day. However, for some conditions homeopathy has its place too, in my experience.

Presence – mindfulness and meditation

Remember I mentioned about the peony unfolding? Well, mindfulness and meditation have helped me gently unfold some of my peony petals.

It was a true gift to listen to my instincts and train in these beautifully wise and powerful techniques. At the point I fully allowed mindfulness and meditation into my life I was fully broken. Crushed. Lifeless. Burned out. Truly at rock bottom. Broken open. This was the point more light got in and I took my healing to a whole other level. It was the next step I was putting in place. It was not based on yelling and screaming, but on my choice to live my personal life in the way I wanted, and a way that was healthy for ME, not how others wanted me to live it.

The westernised approach to mindfulness can be incredibly helpful, although my personal experience is that eastern methods of meditation and Dharma teachings mixed with mindfulness have been more beneficial.

We create such chaos in our worlds and we don't even realise we're doing it because we're going so fast. In my view mindfulness can help us come back to centre where we can begin to learn how to be more aware about what is going on around us, in us, and in the present moment.

I'm a big advocate of Jason Garner's work and he often says …

"It's not about searching for peace but being peaceful with what you find."

This refers to our outer world as well as inner world of course.

For me, meditation practice fuels mindfulness – it's like a figure of eight. Without practising meditation, the mind can't settle and in turn become more aware of what is going on in the present moment, and without mindfulness we don't remember the importance of our meditation practice.

Once we learn to sit and allow what is unhelpful within us to arise, without judging it or following it, just simply observing it, then the power it has over us begins to dissipate.

Let's take the example of fear as mentioned earlier and refer to Jack Kornfield again. When we go into a fear state, we may panic, get angry, cry, etc. However, if we look beyond the story that is causing us to go into a fear state, we can't find fear. Seriously, try and find it – it's not there. What is there is a whole big drama story created by the mind and with our thoughts and habitual behaviour we follow the thoughts instead of being alert to what we can do about the situation.

There are so many benefits to meditation and mindfulness, and plenty of books and resources out there. I personally chose the Kadampa Buddhist tradition as that was where I first came into contact with the notion of meditation back on the school trip when I was eight. It has been so beneficial for me personally and I feel so blessed to have the knowledge of incorporating such wise teachings into my daily life. I don't always get it right of course, and there is plenty for me still to learn, but for me there is no rush either. I learn, I integrate, I put into practice, I fall over often, I pick myself up again and again, I learn, I integrate, I put into practice, and so on.

Bach Flower Remedies

In the 1930s, Dr Bach, a homeopath, researched and created 38 different flower remedies to help bring balance to emotions being experienced by the human. He believed that behind all disease lies our fears, anxieties, greed, likes and dislikes. Heal these emotions and the dis-ease can heal.

He came to understand that when the virtuous vibration of the flowers flood the human energy field the energy can then change. So by changing the frequency of the emotion, the emotion itself has to change.

Courage

I have had to express courage on so many levels. Courage to heal. To be vulnerable. To be intimate. To go internally and dig deep in order to purify. To accept my dad's wishes. To keep getting up after each emotional or mental hit. To sit in stillness with myself and unearth what was there. To allow. To be fully broken open. To admit my failings and be remorseful. To let go of people in my life. To write to my mother and sister and ask if we could begin again. To not give up living. To equalise myself. To sometimes put me first. To have no contact with my mother. To stand up and say, "NO more abuse on any level from anyone". To learn to hold Love for myself. To not be worried when other family members turn their back or go quiet. To sit with others in their pain while they go internally in order to purify too. To ask the difficult yet pertinent questions while holding a space of loving kindness in order that they can heal. To confront pain. To not deviate or give up in the midst of healing despair. To stop being loyal to those who treated me like a rag doll. To accept. To keep an open heart. To be the human I am. To receive. To let the true nature and Integrity of Love flow again. To publish this book. To continue the journey.

I encourage you to allow your courage to surface – you have it – it's within you. You too can heal. Take a deep breath in and allow yourself to walk inwards as well as forwards. The true nature and Integrity of Love will have your back and your true essence can unfold and shine.

Change

If you want change, YOU have to change and that's not always easy. However, I think I have gained the most impactful changes when I have looked at fear head on and said, "Out of my way, I'm coming through!"

Giving up the internal fight or surrendering helped me too, as did allowing things to be as they are. For instance, writing to my sister and mother with deep Love in my being for both, I asked if we could draw a line under our past and move forward acknowledging we had all made mistakes along the way and that can't be changed, but with the present and future in mind we could perhaps come into peace together. My mother said yes, and then sat back to watch things play out not taking any further action, thus triggering my PTSD which manifests in the deepest pain coursing through my heart and a feeling of utter desperation running through my veins as I'm brought to my knees in disbelief. My sister found the fact that I'd initiated the process and was leading it incredibly difficult to come to terms with and so, despite a number of interactions over email and in person, after a time I surrendered to this rather than trying to encourage her to do what she didn't have the capability of doing at that time.

Navigating this fine line can be tricky, especially when emotions can take hold, and I've so often found this difficult to balance as a human. My light body says, "Don't worry, just let them be as they are and don't be ruffled", yet my humanness says I'm hurt by it and I either get angry or I isolate myself. It's taken time, but more often now I've found a balance which keeps me intact and more able to keep an open heart while giving the other person parameters of 'okay-ness' by me as an equal being.

What I did in the instance with my sister is put in place an 'okay-ness filter', that if she is willing to come to the table in peace there is potentially a place to start from, but until then I will not feel guilty for insisting on 'no contact'. It didn't feel loving to me at core and so it was hard to implement, but my sister doesn't have the wherewithal to understand my heart which contains a deep wish for peace for all of us, in other words, Integrity; Wholeness, Honesty Unity, Non-harmfulness.

Ultimately, this filter is a loving action towards me, but also my family as a whole, although it may not seem so right now.

I have made a 'change' in my behaviour and so that produces different results. My family don't particularly like it, I know that, but I rarely get dragged into their drama and chaos these days and I can tell you that is one heck of a relief and nor do I allow myself to feel guilty!

Honesty

I had to be very honest with myself if I wanted to heal and I knew I would need to say it how it was for me on the inside. This was difficult to begin with because not having had a voice that was acknowledged, let alone listened to, in my family, meant I'd shut this down. Also, when making the breakthroughs it would mean I would have to behave differently with regard to my mother and sister and call them on their behaviour towards me. It's interesting how people don't like it when you change. Sadly it can sometimes seem threatening to them.

What being honest with kindness also does is bring the self more into authenticity. This can provide a great deal of relief too. It's like a weight gets lifted from the shoulders.

Learning

I have been like a willing sponge! I have sought out intelligent, ethical therapists, guides and teachers with whom I resonated and who have only been coming from a place of Integrity. I have always wanted to learn how to get the shifts for myself obviously but working in the field I do provides me with the opportunity to share it with others, as and when appropriate.

Life is a journey of learning and we must be open to its continuous path if we are to remain humble.

Determination

Along this healing path I have had a dogged determination to not stop until I can know peace in whatever I find.

"Peace: it does not mean to be in a place where there is no noise, trouble or hard work, it means to be in the midst of all those things and still be calm in your heart." – Anon

I have reached a milestone in that my being is now peaceful on the inside more often than it isn't. It can still be brought off balance if I am not alert and the fire in my belly wants to surge, for instance when I see injustice like selfishness or cruelty to another sentient being. Now though, I am more able to channel my feisty passion and take action while keeping my feet on the ground in order to raise the levels of Integrity present within our planet and especially the human realm.

Often people have seemed to imply that I have been lost – I wasn't and I absolutely knew I wasn't. That used to irritate the hell out of me. I have not been lost on my path, I have simply had a burning desire inside me to not stop purifying and seeking how to share in peace, and what I now know as the true nature and Integrity of Love.

"Not all those who wander are lost" – J.R.R. Tolkien

Recovery from narcissism

My mother has often seemed fragile, insecure and frightened while also being emotionally unavailable – all traits of narcissism. She was, and still is, often not present nor able to offer much in the form of mothership. I do my best to accept this and for the majority of time I can, but my mind challenges me in our relationship and sometimes I fall down and need to remove myself in protection of myself. My mother cannot seem to control herself, so sadly I also have to implement extremely tight boundaries and I choose to do this because I no longer wish to suffer on the end of her selfish behaviour and her choices. Little contact between us is the consequence and sad as it is, that's what she is choosing by not respecting me as an equal human being.

Acceptance has also been key here too though. I've had to work through the realisation that my mother cannot and does not give me Love in the way that is needed from being a child – basic empathy and fundamental pleasing, safety in the form of protection or nurturing advice to help grow inner confidence and a sense of worth and sharing in togetherness as equals.

Narcissism is termed as a mental disorder and the behaviour demonstrated is a form of child abuse. So also realising I had been on the end of abuse from all directions in my family, while not understanding why, has been a real challenge to accept and has taken time to come to terms with. Understanding karma on a deep level helped me take a huge leap forward here.

During this deep work, I have chosen to learn to accept my mother just as she is without needing to change her in any way. I've chosen to stop wishing her to be different than she is and instead accept that she just simply is. I've chosen to accept that my mother cannot flow true Love to me. I've chosen to acknowledge and accept that this goes way back further than my mother and her mother. I've chosen to stop trying to force her to connect more into consciousness and lightness because she is not ready to see it or experience it. In doing so, I found that I can hold Love for her and allow that to flow through me for her. But I have to do this from a distance and not get involved in her daily life. I accept my humanness. This is also where I have come to understand connectedness and separateness at a deeper level. I also learned through KMC and Geshe Kelsang Gyatso Rinpoche's teachings that we only suffer because we want things to be different than they are. Please contemplate this because in the realisation of it there is so much peace.

The other element which really helped me was accepting that narcissists never admit their behaviours and they will NEVER change, because they simply don't see what they don't want to see.

I've also chosen to get over being loyal to my mother for loyalty's sake. When I stopped simply accepting the abusive behaviour she was more often than not subconsciously imparting on me, I was in fact stopping being loyal because that was what was expected from me as a daughter. She is my mother and, of course, I am grateful to her for many things she has done along the way, it wasn't all bad, she gave me life after all, but that does not mean to say I am beholden and have to suffer what she perhaps needs to heal herself.

Narcissism is dark, and I am really determined to highlight its perils because current society is becoming more and more narcissistic – focused on 'me' or 'I' – and I sense it will cause serious disturbance for many as time goes by. It will help us all if we understand this better and I urge you to explore this behaviour in more detail.

Recovery from child sexual abuse

This is a book in and of itself, of course, but I think if I can offer any hope for someone who has been subjected to such abuse, it is to realise that it is in the past. It was so very wrong and absolutely should not have been allowed to happen, but it cannot be changed. You are now in the present moment though and it isn't happening now. That said, if it is happening now – then get yourself safe and tell someone who has the capability to help you, protect you and stop it happening.

Talk to someone you trust. Sharing with someone that it has happened can be a great relief. However, you may want to consider too why you are telling someone if you decide to. Do you simply want the relief of someone else just knowing and someone who will listen to you, or do you want them to help you do something about it? Or do you want helpful strategies for coping in your life today? Choose carefully who you share your pain with. Remember, when I told my mother, she didn't have the capacity to deal with it effectively and that was even more damaging. So I reiterate, choose carefully who you share your pain with.

Connecting to the pain inside can also be helpful and there are techniques such as guided meditations that can be of assistance in the process of 'allowing' the painful feelings and emotions locked in the bodymind to surface. The feelings don't need to be changed, they can arise so they can be felt and then dissipate.

Healing anger

I have been consumed by anger at points in my life. I was in pain. Mostly through feeling hurt by others and blaming them, experiencing and witnessing others not being considerate, of not just me but others too. Also for not having been knowing enough nor strong enough to stand in myself and trust myself and my own instincts, intuition or choices. Frustration has raged and burned within me. Yet, once I began to consciously get a hold of my thoughts around this, things began to shift. To begin with, Reiki helped me enormously as one of its five main principles can be summarised as "Just for today do not get angry". Additionally, and many years later, what helped make a significant difference were Dharma teachings which I found by reading *How to Solve Our Human Problems* by Geshe Kelsang Gyatso Rinpoche and *Love Your Enemies* by Sharon Salzberg and Robert Thurman. The latter book explains about conquering the inner enemy of anger where it is likened to an addiction. So as I worked on my frustration and anger levels, I held in my mind the alcoholic who, wishing to give up alcohol, has to steel themselves not to pick up the bottle or glass of alcohol in order to stay sober. I had to steel myself not to pick up the cup of anger. It is so hard because anger is a rotten habit and comes in many forms, from mild irritation through to full blown manic rage. We follow anger without realising half the time. However, it can be controlled by controlling our thoughts and actions rooted in mind. So basically, shift the mind and anger can shift too. We can give ourselves the gift of patience with ourselves in this process too. What helped me enormously here was a phrase I adopted during my mindfulness training…

With determination at my heart, I begin again with beginner mind.

This can be a good daily practice for all of us, because I'm not sure I know many people who don't at least feel some mild irritation or more during each day.

Action: *Observe and list how many times during one day irritation/anger arises within you. Write down each form of anger, from mild irritation or disgruntlement through to full blown rage. Then begin taming it.*

I think it would be really beneficial, for us all to notice how we are addicted to the habit of anger and we don't even realise it. We just do it without thinking. It's there and even sometimes we argue with ourselves, don't we? I know I do! I have arguments in my head with other people – ranting about how I am angry at their actions! How bonkers is that?! With strong discipline and training in conscious awareness we can reduce this though.

Eckhart Tolle talks about this beautifully in his book *The Power of Now* where he encourages the reader to "watch the thinker". I remember doing this back in 1999 when I first read this wonderful book. I observed myself walking down the street chuntering away to myself in full blown rant (in my head) at my boyfriend of the time – I was doing both sides of the argument too! Do you ever notice yourself doing this? At the point I was able to catch my mind and "watch the thinker" these words went through my mind: "Nutter alert!" This was such normal behaviour for me at that time and yet in that moment it was so apparent how un-present I was and how caught up in the energy of my thoughts I was, without even realising it. It was a day I will never forget as it stopped me in my tracks and I was then able to adjust and begin to move my mind in a more beneficial direction.

Action: *If you can, step back from yourself and "watch the thinker". Notice how many conversations you're having with yourself.*

Action: *With discipline, take control of your thoughts and hold your mind in the present moment as often as you can. I began by using the word "STOP!" to catch myself in mid-flow mind conversation. I then instructed my mind with "I am here NOW, this is NOW, stay here NOW, in this present moment and this moment, and this moment....". Slowly the mind can become disciplined, not to dart off into conversations with itself, but also if it does, then it becomes easier to catch it too. Although at first this may seem difficult, with practice it can become easier.*

Shining true light

Since working in the field of complementary therapies, I have always encouraged others to shine brightly. Without having to do anything, I know my presence (or my light) often irritates people, even people I've only just met. I somehow seem to cause other's stuff to rise to their surface and become apparent, and they don't like it, it irritates them so they then try to pull me down. At points in my life they have managed to for a short time, but not for long.

I encourage you to do the same. If you know in your heart you are standing in Integrity – Wholeness, Honesty, Unity and Non-harmfulness – then you shine as bright as you can and don't let anyone who cannot bear your brightness bring you down. Let them work on dealing with their stuff. You shine brightly!

Queen Evie

How one tiny little dog can give so much joy to so many people while deeply teaching me on my healing journey, I will never know, but she does.

I chose the name Evie because it means 'Breath of Life' in Hebrew and before I got her I thought that's exactly what she would bring to my life. She has done that in spades. My heart sings when I see her almost to the point of joyful tears. It hasn't always been that way though!

During the first year of having her I often thought "What the hell have I done?!" I attended dog obedience classes and the tutor was a fabulous lady, proper old school with Barbara Woodhouse type training methods – we definitely weren't allowed treats to train our dogs. She wanted the dogs to respect their owners, not the treats. So really Chris was helping me too in a new life skill: commanding respect. I wasn't expecting that. It was a struggle to begin with too, but slowly slowly we learned together.

Chris had a wonderful relationship with her German Shepherd dogs and I'll never forget the adoration one of them, Ella, had for her owner when she demonstrated in the class what we then had to do. Needless to say, Evie at that point didn't have the same levels of adoration for me! Chris' method was to teach the owner and the dog, wanting the animal to feel safe while knowing its place too – she was awesome.

Evie was eager to learn, but on her terms of course – most things are on Evie's terms. That's why she is sometimes referred to as Queen Evie! She was cheekily defiant too and Chris used to laugh saying "Remember there is a Rottweiler in there!" That's how much spirit Evie has in her tiny little body.

With a lot of patience and discipline for Evie and me, we got there. I found it difficult and painful to enforce the boundaries I was being taught, namely what is acceptable and what is not. That old chestnut of not wanting another being to go into a position of difficulty or pain too, I only want to take that away and share in Love! However, love and cuddles don't teach; "No, you can't eat that, it's not for you", for example. I had to learn I could teach Evie with Love, but there also had to be a definite "no" in there too and she has to be allowed to be a dog. I didn't always get it right and I still don't, but we have a joyful relationship, bond and beautiful experiences on her walks and outings. I always think of them as her walks as they really are for her. It's her time to be free and wander and smell and explore. It's a complete bonus for me as I too get to experience her joy and the beauties nature has to offer.

I had always been present on our walks – I'd set out with that intention when I first brought her home. However, one day I was in the kitchen – it was during the time I was in the middle of taking some mindfulness training – and she nudged me on the leg with her tiny nose. I crouched down and from my heart to hers asked what she wanted. I was drawn to sit for a while, so I did, I held her in my arms and we just were, in togetherness in those moments for about 20 minutes. Her little body, breath rising and falling as did mine. Her coat soft and wavy. The blackness and yet the soft grey tones too of her hair. Her floppy ears, like a little bit Rastafarian. Her sweet essence being. Her gentle head snuggling into my neck. It was exquisite. I was truly present with her and myself and it was a delightful learning of how it can be when we truly 'be' with another being in the moments. We were in togetherness.

Evie has spirit, and each day I am adoringly grateful for her being in my life and the journey we are on together. I try to do my very best for her and our bond seems to show it goes two ways.

Question: *When you walk with your dog, how often are you in your thoughts, talking to someone else, pushing a pram, doing business on your phone, not present with your dog at all?*

Question: *How often do you notice your dog's gait, how it is smiling, the joy it is having, the smells it is finding? What do you notice about your dog when you walk in togetherness?*

Action: *If you're out walking with your dog, put your phone away and the music or podcast you may be listening to. Be in the presence of your dog on its walk. Feel the earth beneath your feet, notice how you walk and how your dog walks, look at its happiness as it smells each blade of grass even. Learn from your dog. Observe its intelligence. Smell the air that is entering your lungs sustaining your life. It is that same air that sustains the life of all others. Notice your energetic system. See the beauty around you, the nature, the architecture and marvel at how it has been created through the gift of another. Become aware of the universal energy system you exist within. Notice the energy flowing through you. Notice the earth under your feet, which you are connected to each and every day. Slow down and come into being present as you are in the presence of so much incredibleness. This can be how you walk with your dog if you choose it.*

Question: *Similarly, how often are you are actually with the person you are with if you are for instance walking along the street, or in the country, or at the beach?*

Action: *Apply the above actions.*

Question: *How often are you present with yourself as you walk?*

Action: *Apply the above actions.*

Boundaries

As I said, I've had to learn about healthy boundaries into adulthood. With regard to my father and trying to reconnect with him, my counsellor at the time discussed with me a way forward that I was happy with and I call it the "three strikes and you're out rule". I will give anyone a second chance, but after a third time and if things aren't working out equally then that's it, I now place my energies elsewhere, so it is three strikes and you're out. There is no harshness to this, I don't hold any bad feeling towards the other. In the scenario with my dad, I attempted contact with him three times and he didn't want to engage. I don't understand his actions, but as I said I don't hold any harsh feelings towards him. He is entitled to his choices just as we all are, and I simply now respect his wish and get on in my life.

As for my mother, I think you'll understand by now she has no boundaries where I am concerned and so I've tended to implement boundaries in a different way with her, and sadly that sometimes has to include 'no contact'. My mother wants contact with me, but it's not always that healthy for me and my wellbeing because her actions and behaviour towards me is too manipulative. Her wanting contact is more often about her needs than mine, for example her narcissistic supply.

Here is an example during a period of 'no contact'. A couple of months before my birthday, my mother had disregarded my wishes yet again in relation to my sister, so via my step-father I had advised that "I simply have nothing to say to my mother right now" and that was it. They both found this difficult to take, but neither did they ask me any questions about why and how together we could bring peace to the situation and have it resolved.

Anyway, the day of my birthday my mother phoned all sweetness and light to wish me a happy birthday. She was so oblivious and blinkered to my needs and it seemed she couldn't possibly think that I would not want to speak to her on my birthday. I had not expected her to be on the end of the phone, I thought it was probably my step-father phoning, because the insistence of 'no contact' with my mother was in place, so I was quite taken aback, and once again the rug was pulled from under my feet. Now on one level, it could be perceived as kind of my mother to call, but we were on 'no contact' and that's what I had stipulated. Without any thought for me and my wishes, my boundary was trampled once again in total disregard – I was the rag doll once again being flung aside regardless. She can't help herself in her narcissism, you see. SHE wanted to speak to me on my birthday and that's all that mattered, so SHE did, but where was what I wanted in that situation and on my birthday? Nowhere. Where was the thought of equalness? Nowhere. I was then told I was being "harsh" when I reiterated "I have nothing to say". This is a minor example, but you get the picture, right?

Scenarios like this leave me bewildered and with that feeling of being flung around like the rag doll without any regard. Subsequently I will gather myself from the disbelief of my mother's oblivious behaviour (yet again), I will reinstate my boundary, I meditate to bring myself back to centre and connection with consciousness and I move on, letting the experience pass through me. My boundary is reinstated in my mind and I then do my best to hold thoughts of loving kindness for her, holding the wish that one day she will come to know how to be more aware. This can sometimes take me a couple of days, but I do not allow her behaviour and lack of understanding that I am an equal and an adult to render me stuck for longer. It did for years, but not now. This is why I deeply want people to come to understand and be aware of the darkness narcissism creates, and we must bring this to light.

Question: *Do you have your boundaries trampled on and does this cause you pain?*

Action: *What can you do so that you do not get stuck in the pain, but instead can move forward with Love for yourself and hold loving kindness at your heart for the other?*

Question: *Do you trample over others' boundaries and treat others with little regard? If so, why do you choose to do this?*

Question: *What can you do to provide others with kinder regard?*

Action: *Once you have contemplated how you can provide kinder regard to others, then take that action consistently, not just once, but consistently.*

Responsibility

Looking back, I think another great shift happened when I truly acknowledged what I am responsible for, which is clearly most things in my life.

My happiness is nobody else's responsibility – only I can choose to feel that, nobody else can do that for me. My mental health and wellbeing are my responsibility, and if someone else is adversely making that extremely difficult for me to navigate, then it is my responsibility to take control and be the captain of my ship, of my bodymind and my life.

It can be helpful to realise we ourselves are totally responsible for our thoughts. Nobody else is thinking our thoughts for us at any point. People will try and manipulate them, as will companies with their marketing and branding strategies, but WE are responsible for what WE choose to think.

Understanding this can also help take away the need to blame others and in doing so we give ourselves more of a chance to make deep change if we wish for it.

We are also responsible for all our actions. So, if you are heading for burnout for instance, take responsibility for your health and wellbeing now and make appropriate changes to reduce the time you're dedicating to work. If you notice there are patterns in your life such as drinking too heavily, take the reins of responsibility and change your behaviour. Wake up to the notion that everything you are doing is a choice you are making.

In adulthood, nobody else is doing your life for you, only you are.

Creating, then growing and nurturing children in a space of Love and family unity is paramount for them to feel safe, secure and develop confidence. This is the biggest element of responsibility I guess a parent has.

Establishments such as government and schools have certain responsibilities, but they are not responsible for your child/ren's mental health, that is your responsibility as a parent – full stop. Teaching your child/ren moral values is your responsibility. Helping them out of pain in each moment is your responsibility. Creating a home environment for your child/ren that is a stable, safe, peaceful and joyful place in which they can develop and grow is your responsibility. Noticing the true essence of your child/ren and enabling that to flourish is your responsibility. Guiding them and communicating with them openly through the transition from child to teenager to adult is your responsibility. Teaching them about intimacy, what is okay and what is not, is your responsibility. Teaching them about the true nature and Integrity of Love is your responsibility.

Don't ever be too busy or too frightened or too embarrassed to do that, and if you need help with any of it, seek it out. If you do not feel you are able to commit to this, then perhaps give more consideration to becoming a parent.

The word 'responsibility' can be retraced to the word 'respond' which can in turn link to the phrase 'to promise'. So it can be helpful to get conscious about what you promised before you brought your child/ren into the world.

Question: *Did you consciously set out to promise them anything?*

Question: *Are you delivering on those promises?*

Question: *Can you create some promises now?*

Action: *Perhaps consider how you can come back into alignment with the promises you set out to make if you feel you have gone off track. Hold yourself and your child/ren in the space of the true nature and Integrity of Love as you do this.*

Question: *Would it be beneficial in your marital relationship to revisit what you promised each other in taking your vows and any others you have formed along the way?*

How do you Love (remember this means 'to cherish') your child/ren? That doesn't mean spoil with material items, nor manipulate them into doing what you want to do, or want them to do for their best without knowing what is their best from their essence point of view? How do you see them in each moment? Why have you had child/ren if for instance you 'choose' to then leave them in the care of someone else for the most part of the week perhaps because you feel it's less fulfilling to you bringing up children than the fulfilment you get from employment? Controversial question perhaps – I'm not judging you – I just hear many mother's say, "I don't feel like I'm doing anything fully". So I'm simply asking a question, so you can step back and ask it of yourself with the true nature and Integrity of Love in your heart, i.e. Wholeness, Honesty, Unity, Non-harmfulness. How does this encourage them into that space of Love too? Are you too tired by the end of the week to really engage with them? Will the iPad be a better form of Love for your child than looking into your eyes that see them not through blurry exhaustion or wishing to be elsewhere, or irritation because you're thinking about something else, but with the purity of Love as you hold that gaze. If you're too busy or caught up in your life to do that then perhaps contemplate ditching some of the other stuff.

Apologise sincerely

Not acknowledging how we have hurt another can cause so much pain for them. This is a balance though, understanding that the other is choosing to feel hurt, but also accepting we have a responsibility not to cause harm if we are coming from a place of Integrity. Apologising from the heart and then repeating the same behaviour is fruitless and only causes harm. However, choosing to apologise sincerely and then behaving differently because you are mindful that the previous way causes another harm can contribute to rebuilding trust and therefore create more peace and harmony for yourself as well as the other.

This does not, however, mean we become a doormat for another to walk on so we are taken advantage though. We can at all times hold our self in equalness. As I said, this is a fine balance and takes skill to navigate, but it is possible.

Question: *Is there something you can sincerely apologise for, even if it goes back a long time?*

Action: *While holding a space of loving kindness, can you apologise sincerely and with the intention of breaking down resistance and creating more harmony and trust, and therefore allowing the true nature and Integrity of Love to flow more freely?*

Action: *Can you let go of your ego and apologise sincerely, while also needing nothing in return nor holding an expectation of how the other will respond or not? This is pure giving by the way.*

Question: *If someone apologises sincerely to you, can you truly forgive them and let it go?*

Non-judgemental awareness

Learning more about this during my mindfulness teacher training was inspirational.

My understanding is that judgement implies just a set of pictures and words or thoughts that arise within awareness. These may form in a positive, negative or neutral light. Obviously, we have to make judgements and they can be helpful, such as judging a child's actions which may be inappropriate or dangerous, for example if they are too near a fire and you have to educate them accordingly, setting boundaries for them to develop and flourish happily. Some people may suffer depression and make judgements to take action preventing them from spiralling down further. Others may make judgements on whether a new job is a positive move or not, and so on.

However, coming into a place of non-judgemental awareness means refraining from judgement based on our own personal ethical standards or opinions. So we then suspend our thoughts and just 'be' in that moment with what is. (Clearly, I'm not talking about if we are in a dangerous situation here – scarper if you need to!) This, however, is not as simple for we humans as it is written here unfortunately. We have been taught to label almost everything and so we are ingrained in this habitual pattern. Let me explain a bit more.

Left alone the brain will automatically judge things:

- Good/bad
- Right/wrong
- Fair/unfair
- Important/unimportant
- Urgent/non-urgent
- Like/dislike

It happens so fast it's as if it's automated. It's often based on a past teaching or experience, not the present. Being mindful, coming from a space of non-judgemental awareness in the moment, can bring in a fresh perspective.

So when we bring in awareness rather than judgement, things can change for us. For example:

- Be aware of stress or tension. Instead of thinking I'm aching or I have so much tension, just be aware. It's not good/bad/painful, it's just your body doing what it is doing. Also notice that when the mind is distracted in other ways, more often than not we do not notice the aching pain.
- Observe your thoughts in your mind, such as frustration or anger. Again, it's not good or bad, it is what is arising. Instead of following the frustration and going into anger, don't judge it but do observe it like a hawk. I find the words "That's interesting I'm thinking that" can be helpful at this point. Nothing more, nothing less, just "That's interesting". It causes the pause.
- Instead of trying to change ourselves from being a failure to being successful, begin to accept yourself in the moment just as you are and simply connect with your essence. 'Be' in the moment in the you that is.
- Put the stick down, stop beating yourself up. There is no need to battle anymore and continue the internal fight. Just be aware of the present moment, not judging whether you are good or bad, right or wrong. Just being aware brings you into the present.
- Consider not judging one tree as prettier than another – just notice them in their essence.
- Notice that each animal has their role in nature – not making one more or less than another. We are all equal, and as humans we are animals too of course, part of the ecological system.
- Think of a spider. Why judge it as having to be scary? You enable the spider to have power over you – why are you choosing to do that? Observe the spider and hold Love in your heart for it simply as part of nature just like you are – nothing more, nothing less. Suspend judgement on all else to do with the spider.

- Stop criticism of others. Stop putting labels on. Stop disliking or liking. Suspend judgement and just allow that person to be as they are. If they speak and it irritates you, for now stop judging the other person and instead turn to work on your own stuff, starting with the sensation of irritation and contemplate why you're choosing to be irritated and find where that irritation lies.
- Stop categorising – for example, he's boring and quiet, or he's too loud and always has something to say or an opinion, couldn't he just listen for once?! He is what/who he is and he's on his journey, just like you are. Question yourself as to why you have the need to want to change him?
- Become aware of that person – give them open space within your heart. We have so many opportunities to develop loving kindness and compassion towards others …

So at the beginning of this book I asked you to suspend judgement on the people I refer to. I made a real point of this because they too are simply on their journeys, just like you and I are on ours. They are equally valid in their being, just like you and I are too. Everyone has their story going on inside them and there is no one that is pain free – although they may not exhibit that. That is their choice.

To my mother's best friend, my mother is wonderful. To my nephews, my sister is their mum whom they Love. Just because I have difficulties with them does not make them inherently bad – they are not. Nobody handed my parents a manual on how to be a good mother and father – perhaps we all need to contemplate this a bit more and question why with all our human intelligence we have not come to understand generally as a species the importance of providing loving, cherishing, confident parenting. My mother's mother was apparently an extremely difficult women, and no doubt she suffered at the hands of her parents – how far do you go back? We have all suffered and in my view we all have our different karma to purify. We are all just getting through life as best we can with the resources we have available, and so may I encourage you to be less harsh on others, drop down into your heart centre and just be in awareness, rather than judging.

Let us not waste time judging each other, but instead let us learn how we can all more easily bring into our lives the true nature and Integrity of Love for ourselves and those around us.

Acceptance and resistance

There is much out there about acceptance and this can form an important part of the journey to heal, but my goodness it can be such a difficult element to come to terms with.

I found differentiating between acceptability and acceptance was quite key. These are two ends of a seesaw. For me acceptability equates to boundaries or parameters, whereas acceptance equates to being peaceful with what you find. Acceptance certainly does not mean condoning everything but being peaceful inside and then addressing matters appropriately with positive action, for the benefit of all wherever possible.

Examples of acceptability might be: standards of work, for instance parameters of what is okay to pass quality control. Another example might be: you have an agreement with your partner that it is acceptable to each of you to do separate activities on Tuesday evenings. You may also let someone know that if they want to be in your life then certain behaviour is not acceptable, such as heavy drinking if you have a history of attracting alcoholics as partners and you want to change that aspect of your life. If you run a children's group activity, then kindness to all is acceptable, bullying of others is not … and so on.

Examples of acceptance might be: being peaceful with what you find, such as when your train is delayed. You cannot control that, so being anything other than peaceful about it is pointless. You can of course take action, such as contacting your partner to let them know you'll be late or taking another form of transport.

Understanding this difference helped me stop the doormat behaviour I was prone to displaying.

Accepting others as they are has in general been easier for me than accepting myself as I am. I think many people will understand this.

For me it has been so difficult because of the narcissistic abuse, which causes the child wanting to desperately 'please' the narcissist and therefore channel 'Love' rather than the darker, more hateful behaviour and energy. This encourages more harmony and of course the narcissist receives the narcissistic supply they so crave. In doing so, the abused one ends up feeling that who they are and what they do is never enough. It's utterly cruel, but once worked through to understanding, healing can occur and accepting the self just as you are can arise.

Understanding my humanness was a huge relief too and Jason Garner's writings helped me enormously here. It was like a huge weight was lifted from my shoulders. I didn't have to try and be perfect anymore. I could simply accept myself just as I am.

Accepting that I don't particularly resonate with my family, that I am very different from my mother and sister in the way I think and behave – that is okay for me and them. I'm not awkward or difficult, just different. That was a big relief too.

Accepting that things are as they are was another breakthrough. Knowing I can either take action or choose not to.

Accepting the sexual abuse had happened to me and I couldn't change that. As I've mentioned this was a huge breakthrough. The fight inside me stopped and I reside in peace regarding this.

Accepting people as they are. This does not necessarily mean you condone all their behaviours or have to constantly engage with them if you are feeling harmed by them; what it means is you let go of the need to try and manipulate or change them into how you want them to be or behave. You will notice the fight inside you falls away when you are able to do this.

Accepting that this is the life I'm living and I am now more often consciously choosing what happens within it. Huge awakening!

…and so on…

Internal resistance is a great indicator of our mind swimming upstream so to speak, completely in the opposite direction of the flow of the true nature and Integrity of Love. When we STOP and then pause to contemplate what we are resisting and where that is residing in the bodymind, we can then allow the resistance to arise and be in acceptance of what we're finding. This can often be challenging for us because 'fear', for instance, might arise. However, as mentioned earlier, Jack Kornfield explains through Dharma teachings about this so beautifully when he says you can't find fear if you look for it properly. There is the 'drama of the story' but fear doesn't exist. With this in mind, it can sometimes make it less challenging to confront our resistances. It can also be beneficial to hold a space for the true nature and Integrity of Love to flow through and around us as we face our resistances, so they can dissipate, and we are able to advance further along the path of acceptance.

When working through coming more readily to a place of acceptance, it can be helpful to ask the self:

What am I resisting?

Question: *What are you resisting in your life right now, and for what purpose? Is it your ego perhaps at play or not?*

Action: *Choose to stop resisting if you can, and instead allow yourself to pause and be and whatever it is to come into your awareness. So, for example, when something minor gives rise to feelings of anger, ask yourself "What am I resisting and what am I not accepting?"*

I think it's also important to mention here about knowing when non-acceptance is ok.

If you are in danger, you do not have to accept it. Physical abuse, for instance, is never ok, neither is sexual abuse and neither is mental abuse, such as narcissism, enslavement, etc. It is perfectly acceptable to indicate non-acceptance of these behaviours by removing yourself from them. By removing yourself it does not mean you won't have internal work to you do, you will. What it will do though is create space to have some peace and rebuild yourself.

Self-care

Self-care for me is not about going to a spa or buying a new item of clothing. For me, it is being aware of self-alignment; what feels good in my heart will mean I'm relaxed in my beingness. So in my view being authentic with no performance is a real act of self-care.

For example, I believe all beings are equal and all life deserves due regard. I thought I always did my best to treat all beings equally. However, when I truly woke up to the fact I was unconsciously happily eating animals and coproducts from them I saw that I wasn't really aligned to compassion for all living beings, and it was a horrific wake-up call. I felt like I'd been blind and ignorant before I began eating in the vegan way, as I hadn't really contemplated deeply the life and death of animals that ended up on my plate and in my cup. However, with self-care in mind, I simply realised I'd now woken up and could take action more aligned to my beliefs with more awareness. I didn't need to beat myself up. Nor did I try and fix the past – that would be way too tricky! I just let all that go and simply came one step closer into alignment at my heart.

Another example of self-care is that I shield myself from what I interpret as my mother's lack of wherewithal and obliviousness when I need to. I also acknowledge that I perhaps still have some inner work to do here and I will do that in my own time as and when it feels right intuitively for me, no one else.

Question: *What are your core values and are you taking actions that consistently align with them?*

Action: *Write down what your essence is, what you value in your life and how you wish to express your true nature, such as your compassion, kindness, liveliness, fun, extravagance, etc. Then do it – align your behaviours and heart in wholeness, come from a place of true Integrity.*

Equalness

This term may seem strange to some, but I prefer it to that of, for example, equality, which to me can often feel charged with fight, e.g. people are fighting for equality. That to me does not feel like it incorporates the true nature and Integrity of Love within it, but instead that protection in some form is still needed. In my view, when we come from a place of equalness we are offering it as well as holding ourselves in it and that feels more peaceful in my heart. I also heard a long time ago from one of my friends, a beautiful soul and my gentle rock, that when 'ness' is added to the end of a word and it seems to become a made-up word, angels are speaking to us – and I thought that quite delightful.

One of the moments I realised my equalness was when I told my mother, "You are no better nor worse than me and I you. Nor are you greater nor lesser than me and I you. We are equal." Every living being is equal – we may not always realise it, but we are all living side by side together and we all have a place in the nature that is this earth – we are all contributing to it.

Action: *Realise that we are all equal. This can be an extremely humbling moment if you feel it through your heart.*

Action: *Similarly, you are no less than any other being, nor more than any other being – simply equal. Realise that too.*

So a child's essence is equal to an adult's essence, which is equal to the essence of a dog, a cow, an ant, a tree, a flower, a man, a woman, gender neutral, a chief executive, a cleaner, a car driver, a cyclist, a mother, a father, a person of faith, a person of non-faith, and so on. FORGET THE LABELS, WE ARE ALL SIMPLY EQUAL IN HAVING LIFE. No more than each other and no less than each other, purely equal. Wake up! We all breathe the same air and without it, NONE of us exist.

Let us come to realise this fully in our hearts and accept that the true nature and Integrity of Love flows through and around all of us indiscriminately. So why are we causing discrimination on any level?

Question: *What or who are you not treating equally? Include yourself of course.*

Question: *Do you favour one child more than another, not meaning to, but it just seems to happen? Or indeed it is easier to do so?*

Question: *What can you do to bring in more equalisation to your thoughts and behaviours?*

Action: *If you operate with a 'doormat' behaviour tendency, by lowering your worth for instance, instead bring yourself into equalness. You are equal, come to know this at your heart.*

Action: *Stand in front of a mirror and say to the person looking back, "We are all equal, I am equal".*

Essence and spirit

I understand that our pure essence is light energy and consciousness. However, in this human life my essence is to bring healing to the fore for myself and others – I know this in the depths of my heart. My essence is also a quiet warrior at heart too. A warrior of truth, of reaching peace inside and with that which I find on the outside. I am not perfect and don't always get things right and still need to work on stuff of course, but I do know my essence and it is loving, healing, intuitive, kind, caring, loyal, compassionate, careful, fair and a little bit shy. My spirit is alive, quirky, funny, curious, creative, feisty, determined, as well as a bit grumpy at times. It is more at ease being fluid, free and not contained, preferring the outdoors and fresh air, quietness and a gentle pace.

Question: *What is the essence of you, and at this point I'm not talking of the love and light elements?*

Action: *Sometimes, it can help to think of the question, "If I were an animal, what animal would I be?" It may help us to notice our tendencies. For example, a lion will be a very different essence to a dolphin.*

Question: *Ask your child, if they were an animal what would they be? This can be fun but also quite revealing too.*

The word 'essence' stems from 'to be' so I'm referring to your beingness, who you are in the depths of your being and that which lives in the human form, the beingness that when it is enabled to blossom it utterly unfolds and flourishes. Are you creative, are you not, are you practical, are you not, are you intellectual or are you not? Are you a giver or not? Are you quiet or shy or vivacious? Allow yourself to follow your natural nature, not that which you think you should. 'Should' carries a heavy feeling more often than not, and that can be a good indicator you're not connected to your essence. Sift through what it is that shines most brightly in your being. There will be red herrings, but if you are to more easily flow in your life then allow the grace of your beingness and true essence. Come into authenticity.

Action: *Really know your spirit and essence and align with it and live from that. It can be like a weight lifts from your shoulders.*

When I was five, I vividly remember being asked what I wanted to be when I grew up. I also distinctly knew that I wanted to be Father Christmas! I also distinctly remember the surprise for the adult who asked me that question. They also asked me why I wanted to be Father Christmas, so with utter conviction, I promptly replied: "I want to make everyone happy and if I give them presents they'll be happy."

So here is my gift to you, and just like back when I was five, from deep within my essence I hope that by reading this, the happiness you experience will be through connecting to consciousness, the true nature and Integrity of Love and its flow. I deeply wish this for you, and especially your growth into continued peace and joy, as well as all those other beings you cross paths with. It will also have a ripple effect. The more you align with the true nature and Integrity of Love, the more others will be able to open to it too, so may the gift be passed on.

As for interacting with others, we can simply acknowledge that our essence is potentially very different from that of any siblings you may have. Similarly, if you have more than one child, their essences will be different from each other.

Question: *Do you more often bind your children together in their essence because time is limited or it's easier? Or do you allow them the freedom of expression and nudge it along in the direction of a path appropriate and in alignment for them as individuals – not you, but them?*

Take time to sit together in your child's essence – experience their energy, see their pressures and the imprints they are receiving and creating, and perhaps those which are not benefitting them fully. Be gentle with yourself if you realise you are causing them difficulty. Communicate with them and hear them deeply, don't just listen with half of you, and don't be waiting to speak if another person is expressing themselves. Don't feel the need to act upon justifying yourself either. Have courage, be present; hold Love in your heart and hold a safe space; include yourself in that space.

Question: *What is the essence of your child/ren?*

Question: *What is his/her natural nature and spirit?*

Question: *How does their energy work?*

Question: *How do they understand your messaging and you theirs? Is it clear or not?*

Question: *What life will suit their essence? Consider this deeply and in communication with them.*

Question: *How can the essence of your child/ren be developed and expanded so they are not disrupted and guided in the wrong direction?*

Action: *Let your child/ren's natural essence flourish, don't dampen their spirit. Really understand and know the spirit and essence of your child/ren from your heart centre and guide that. They will forge ahead in life and authenticity if you do.*

Action: *You can do the above with your partner, family and friends too – come to understand your essences, spirits and energies.*

Realigning self with essence

Once I had reconnected with my essence, I could begin to realign with it and come more into my central core being. I could access my intuition more easily and being Carmen became simple and less tiring again. When we move away from our core essence, we go off track in life and it becomes more complicated than it needs to be.

Question: *Are you aligned with your core essence?*

Question: *If not, what would help you reconnect and therefore realign with your core essence? Ask your heart or perhaps meditate on it.*

Question: *Do you act upon your intuition?*

Question: *If not, what is stopping you?*

I made a humdinger of a mistake not too long ago, but it taught me hugely on this level. I felt pretty aligned to my core essence and intuitively knew a move would be good for me, but I held off and went back into my old behaviours of fear and lack of confidence, listening to others instead of myself. It's like echoes were being sounded in my life as I played them out. I missed a really good opportunity. I didn't follow my intuition and the ease of how things were unfolding in my life, however, I have now got the message big time regarding this. Never again will I not trust myself when my essence is speaking to me so directly, so I guess all was not lost on this occasion.

Question: *Are you taking action which is not in line with your intuition?*

Question: *If so, where is it taking you?*

Action: *Take action in line with your intuition – the deep knowing at your core. It feels whole when you connect with it and that you are coming from a place of the true nature and Integrity of Love. That doesn't mean to say it will always be sparkly and beautiful, sometimes acting from intuition means facing our fears and walking towards them head on, but it feels peaceful and congruent at the heart centre when we do. We can then let this guide us, checking in and ensuring it is aligned to the true nature and Integrity of Love.*

Understanding my mind

It's complex yet simple too. What I learned in classes at the Kadampa Meditation Centre in London helped me calm my mind further and that has been invaluable. It helped me begin to understand its workings:

"At any time my mind can take me to the moon, but my body can't go there." – Geshe Kelsang Gyatso Rinpoche

My mind is not in my head but resides in my heart if I discipline it to do so and this takes practice, but the more I practise the easier it gets.

My mind and ego can take me places it's not necessary to go to, yet it can also take me into exquisiteness.

We need to be constantly aware and alert to where our minds take us.

I still have so much to learn on this subject and will do along the rest of my journey, I don't doubt.

Meditation can be a wonderful tool to help us bring our minds more into consciousness and, in so doing, we become present, more able to discipline our mind, to move it rather than it just taking us where it wants to go.

The past is the past

Stop trying to fix the past. Many of us try to do this, going over in our minds, trying to make it something it wasn't, addressing the wrongs done to us, chewing over if I'd done this, if only they'd done that, and so on. I did this for years myself, but the past is the past, we can't change it, and it is nonsense to even contemplate it in our heads apart from if we are trying to assess how to do things differently from now on.

The past is for two things: reminiscing fondly over and learning from.

Authenticity

'Authentic' can be traced to the Greek words meaning 'author' and 'master' and I like this translation within the context of this book. Therefore, may I ask you to encourage your child/ren to grow within their authenticity. Not what the being they feel they ought to be or the façade they have to live behind, the false version of them they must portray so they are thought the best of, and so on.

If your child is shy – they are. If your child is quiet – don't try and make them loud because you find it uncomfortable that they're not. I believe the best gift you can give your child is gentle confidence within themselves and their essence, while living within the realms and connected to the true nature and Integrity of Love.

Yes, teaching maths is important, but we can teach our children so much more. How about teaching them how to manage their money? How about teaching compassion and what peace truly is? How about teaching what it is to communicate harmoniously? How about teaching what it is to stand in the shoes of others and view the world from their shoes and heart? How about teaching the footprint of where each item of each meal in a given day comes from and what is involved? How about teaching how to simply co-habit with our planet, what Integrity is, how to accept ourselves and others just as we are, to understand we are all different, to give due regard to all beings that we come into contact with, to be grateful in our hearts, what Love is and isn't, and so on? Do our children not get caught up in a lot that is unnecessary?

If you are tired of being in a performance of your life – change it. If you work in IT and yet you yearn to do something else – do it! If you have always wanted to run your own business – do it! If you want to travel – do it! You are the author and master of your life, remember.

The relief of being your authentic self can release a heavy weight. It also provides support for growing confidence. It is like an outer layer of clear film is taken off and you can reveal your true essence.

Questioning integrity

As I implied right at the start of this book, one of my wishes is that we raise the Integrity bar within the human species. It is going to be a tough job because Integrity seems to be lacking in so many areas of daily life. However, as an individual you now have the awareness of the true nature of what Integrity is, and the wisdom is within you to use it. So may I ask you join me and take action to assist all humans in helping raise the Integrity bar. We will need to show courage and patience to begin with, but let us at least try.

Action: *Whenever Integrity is not present (including within yourself), may you gently highlight it, while of course holding a space of loving kindness as you do – simply allowing the true nature and Integrity of Love to flow as you gently bring others to the understanding of what it is.*

Understanding it's an inside job

It is no one else's job except your own to heal your own stuff. That's the way I look at it. We can blame, hate, fight, be angry at others, but that changes nothing. The transformation of those emotions can only happen on the inside and the purification of the emotions and thoughts can be done by nobody else but ourselves.

Here's how easy it is, but we humans make it so difficult, including me – it's laughable really!

And I simply decided to be happy again.

…a continuing journey…

I have had an incredible journey to date and can now give a hug of Love to myself, with Love for myself. I have found my integral self, or I should say I have allowed my true essence to be revealed again. I am not perfect and nor do I have all the answers; I have said from the off that I don't profess to that, but coming through what I have and being able to connect to the true nature and Integrity of Love in the moment now gives me much peace. I no longer feel a failure, I no longer feel inauthentic having to put on a performance. It is a deep relief. The essence of me that was dampened and oppressed now shines brightly again. I am free, and in that freedom I acknowledge my humanness. I no longer do what other people think I should, nor even think I must adhere to what I think others are thinking because that is utterly bonkers! I often reconnect to a phrase I learned during my Reiki training:

What other people think of me – good, bad or neutral – is none of my business, because I will never 100% know.

I am perfectly imperfect and all my heart wishes to do is be in joy, continue purifying and take actions that align with the compassion in my heart and the true nature and Integrity of Love. I practise diligently staying present and I will practise this to my death, because it is a practice and I choose it. I believe that's part of my journey, and I wish to travel that path. It gives me great pleasure knowing my essence and truly connecting with it, and I wish for everyone else to connect into this conscious space of being too.

"The real revolution is the evolution of consciousness" – The Spiritual Vegan

We are all on our own journey. There will always be things to face and more opportunities to make mistakes and learn. Healing and purifying are possible if we choose it and the true nature and Integrity of Love is always there to support us. Have courage, be gentle with yourself, and be open to continuous learning and growth.

Part 6: The Wider Picture

The wider picture

This takes into consideration:

- Forget the world of 'Me & I'
- Compassion for all
- Compassion in action
- Let us bring an end to violence
- What's the rush?
- Truly sharing Love

Forget the world of 'Me & I'

This is what the world of narcissism looks like. The world of 'Me & I' is hideous and dark. I want, I need, this is mine, I think it should be like this or that, it's my way or the highway, I'm first get out of my way, I'm more important than another, my family is better than yours, my view is more important than yours, my religion is more important than yours, my colour deserves xyz, because I'm this identity I deserve xyz way more than you … and the list goes on.

WE ARE ALL EQUAL IN OUR BEINGNESS and we can share in the true nature and Integrity of Love. Every being on this land breathes the same air and without it we are nothing.

Action: *Pause to contemplate that … "Every being on this land breathes the same air and without we are nothing." We are equal, not better or more than another, and we are not worse or less than they are.*

You breathe and I breathe, the cat breathes as does the ant as does the cow as does the bird as does the tree. Let us lift up and come to live more with compassion for all, equally, peacefully, sharing in kindness, joy and happiness. Help each other be and notice the jewel and incredibleness inside of a.n. other in the moment rather than noticing what you don't think they are, or how they are irritating you. Control yourself and open your heart to Love in that moment instead. If you're in the board room and there is £50,000 up for grabs, ask which department needs it most, not how can I get my hands on it for MY department – you're all working for the same cause after all, right? Stop pushing and pulling, and instead start giving. We are all under one roof essentially and that is called gravity. Let us at least abide in Integrity.

Compassion for all

During the winter of 2017, I read a post on social media from dog owners whose tiny pup Angus had run off in Richmond Park, London. For three nights this little 14-week-old pup survived out in what must have seemed like the wilderness with temperatures below freezing. Social media enabled many people to be aware and they went out searching for him. On the 4th day I drove up from Surrey at 7am before work to also contribute and search. I happened to meet the owners who were distraught and desperate to find their newest family member. The pain they were experiencing was palpable. We walked together and I encouraged them to keep open to him being found, after all, so many people were searching. Later that day he was found curled up in a tree trunk – it was a beautiful miracle.

That little dog caused so much compassion to be demonstrated and he certainly sowed a seed in my heart. The true nature and Integrity of Love flowed through people as they searched for Angus on behalf of his owners. He really opened hearts.

Totally separately or so I thought(!), later in 2017 I began to feel that something wasn't quite right with my consuming dairy – I couldn't put my finger on it, but I began to know that I needed to reduce my dairy intake. I couldn't understand these thoughts but as I began to look at things more consciously and noticed I consumed a lot of milk and cheese in my diet.

A friend of mine suggested I consider doing a 22-day programme run by *www.challenge22.com* It does what it says on the tin – it's a 22-day challenge of eating vegan. It is encouraged that you hook up the support group via Facebook where they provide online support from mentors, dieticians and you're part of a community all in the same boat and giving the 22-day challenge a go. I had never considered being vegan and I had a lot of judgements attached to what it was, and you guessed it, these were all based on what others said. Until I connected with my friend Johanna, I didn't know any vegans. However, when I look back there had been flashes of 'veganism' trying to catch my attention in the previous six months. I met a couple of vegans on holiday, a client of mine said she might try going vegan, and so on. So I decided to give it a go in a very casual manner, thinking if I at least reduce my dairy intake over that 22 days it will be interesting to see if I notice any differences, and I didn't eat much honey, meat or poultry anyway. Fish was a no-no so that wouldn't be difficult!

During the first week of the challenge a couple of film documentaries were brought to my attention. The first was *www.meat.org* and the second was *www.landofhopeandglory.org* – both similar in the fact that they educated me on the brutal reality of animal agriculture, particularly factory farming, and the killing methods of the farmed animals. Both films were traumatising to watch but both were showing the truth of what goes on behind such closed doors. There was no element of compassion in what had been filmed. I was horrified. Not only because of the amount of suffering and terror the animals were subjected to during their living days, but also the horrific nature of how they were killed and the processes their bodies were put through on behalf of humans, so they could eat them purely to satisfy their taste buds. I was doubly horrified because I had been doing this and never had the wherewithal to look into it or contemplate how the steak on my plate had arrived there. It didn't even enter my radar. I am the granddaughter of a farmer and I am sure my grandfather would be horrified by some of the methods used in farming today. I was brought up being told meat, chicken, dairy, honey, fish were all good sources of food and nourishment. What shocks me hugely about myself though is that I never ever thought to question or educate myself as to whether this was honest or true, let alone compassionate! I simply trusted in what I was taught. Possibly because I was just treading water with plenty of other things to navigate, but when I did open my heart and mind, while being willing to also open my eyes and watch footage of the horrors inflicted in the agricultural industry, I could not un-see what I'd witnessed, and neither could I ignore it. I vowed I would never again be part of that for the sake of the non-human animals, for the sake of the people I had inadvertently been asking to kill on my behalf, for the sake of my health and for the sake of the planet.

I have been vegan ever since and gratefully so – it was like a switch flicked inside me. I realised I wasn't being compassionate to all. The vegan way of life is simply a compassionate way of living all round, and as much as possible considers equalness of all. You can be an unhealthy vegan of course, but I've chosen to eat as naturally as I can. I'm healthier on many levels including physically, mentally, emotionally and ethically by choosing to be vegan and it seems more beneficial from an environmental perspective too. However, I would like to understand more about human practices and Integrity where plant farming is concerned.

As humans, we are naturally compassionate beings – allow your true essence to flow as there is nothing about killing animals for food as we currently do which involves the true nature and Integrity of Love.

Question: *Do you understand deeply how these animals do not want to die? They simply want to live in peace, just like you and I.*

Question: *Would you yourself have the capacity to kill each being that comes onto your plate?*

Question: *If not, have you considered that because you won't, you have caused someone else to have to, and many of these people who work in slaughterhouses end up with mental health problems including PTSD?*

Question: *Is that fair and does any of that contain the true nature and Integrity of Love?*

Question: *Do you know that the human colon is two-thirds longer than that of a carnivore? This means a carnivore can flush out quickly any meat it eats, whereas humans cannot, and so that rotting flesh takes much longer to pass through the human gut.*

Action: *Contemplate, be curious and educate yourself on how your body works and functions, particularly from a gut perspective. A healthy gut provides a healthy being, a leaky gut does not.*

Action: *Contemplate what is on your plate, the footprint of it and whether or not you need it to survive.*

Action: *Show compassion to yourself and contemplate deeply the food you put into your body, not only where it has come from, but how it nourishes your cells, or if it doesn't.*

Action: *Consider watching the film documentaries and doing the 22-day challenge or something similar if you are drawn to it. Obviously, if you are on serious medications you would need to change your dietary habits in communication with your physicians. The statistics are out there though, and a plant-based diet is proven to help reduce heart disease, diabetes and cancers.*

"Until he extends his circle of compassion to all living things, man will not himself find peace" - Albert Schweizer

At the time of writing, I have only been vegan for a year, but I have benefitted enormously. My heart has been opened vastly, I know I am even more compassionate. Physically, my body aches less as it seems less inflamed by the ingested animal hormones coursing round it. I sleep well and wake up with a spring in my step instead of hauling myself out of bed. My mood is lighter. My skin is no longer dry. I simply feel better emotionally, mentally and physically.

I truly believe that by getting clear in my body, the ability for the true nature and Integrity of Love has been able to flow more easily through me.

When we consider others and take action for their highest good and greatest joy in their heart, we are not self-focused, and what comes with that is a deep feeling of goodness that words can't explain. I'm sure you have all had that at some point in your life, right? In my belief, that is an experience of the true nature and Integrity of Love flowing through us.

Wholeness is being experienced, pure honesty and unity too, while no element of harmfulness present. Nothing within you feels edgy or wrong or uncertain, nor is there any element of darkness or harm. You simply know in your heart it is truth and there is lightness. That is an expression of the true nature and Integrity of Love.

So all you need to do is keep asking "What would the true nature and Integrity of Love do?"

Compassion in action

Compassion in action can be more outwardly focussed and so in general doesn't include intentions and behaviours which include "I want, me, myself, me, I, forget him, forget her, me, I, my success, my achievement, my family forget theirs". In these self-orientated behaviours what is really arising here is the sense of "Ego, I will feed you whatever" and your ego sits there laughing as it slips and slides around you, manipulating you at every possible opportunity. Starve it by simply considering others and taking action to benefit them. This will bring you more into accessing the true nature and Integrity of Love in the moment. Take action with compassion as the root intention and you will provide incredibleness. Your ego will fight you as it begins to lose its grip, but stay strong, you can feed compassion instead.

Question: *How can you yourself take compassionate action considering others? Contemplate this.*

Action: *If you're a successful businessperson, could you perhaps mentor someone who in their current conditions doesn't have a chance but does have the drive?*

Action: *If you're naturally a compassionate dad – could you give an hour a week to charity to help children that don't have one present in their lives? Or even set up a support group to teach young men what it is to be a compassionate dad, so they can share that with their child/ren.*

Action: *If you're a dog lover, notice how you might be differentiating between species by loving dogs and yet eating chickens for instance. Instead can you open your heart wider to encompass all non-human animals and align your heart and morals fully with your actions. Consider not being speciesist.*

Action: *If you are more fortunate than someone else in any way, shape or form (which you will be) take action and share what you can.*

Action: *Help others with your actions, not just your money. Remember the kind dentist from my childhood. He didn't give us money – he gave us a roof and a home, something we really needed.*

Action: *Be compassionate to yourself too. If for example you are low on inner resource, take some time to do what you need to in order to rebuild it and don't feel guilty. If you operate a little bit with doormat behaviour tendencies, get support to strengthen your inner resolve.*

Action: *Keep asking, "What would the true nature and Integrity of Love do?" because what the dentist did was act on what the true nature and Integrity of Love would do.*

Let us bring an end to violence

There is so much violence going on in the world currently even on a basic level, and it is up to we humans to end it. Until we are prepared ourselves as individuals to make a stand, draw a line in the sand and only think from a place of the true nature and Integrity of Love, violence will have a place in our societies. We must take responsibility for it happening, even if we do not think we are contributing to it. On some level, we will be if we are not coming from Wholeness, Unity, Honesty, Non-harmfulness for all beings, in other words, from the heart that has the Integrity of Love flowing through it.

As a group consciousness we do have the power to end violence, but that cannot be done through violence on any level, even for instance sniping at each other. The only way we can contribute to this is to choose and decide to draw a line in the sand NOW. And from this moment forward, with all the will in your being, discipline your mind into coming from a place of the true nature and Integrity of Love. In every given situation you possibly can, say to yourself, "What would the true nature and Integrity of Love do right now?" and then act on that. Teach your children to ask themselves, "What would the true nature and Integrity of Love do?" so they too can then act upon it. If your child/ren then pull you up with "Mum/Dad – what would the true nature and Integrity of Love do?" be graceful, surrender your ego and then act from that space of Love.

For the sake of the planet and all those within it, we can do this, we can conquer our thoughts of fear, anger and violence and bring more peace, Love and Integrity to this world. Love energy will support us in the process and we can let that force surge forward through us.

What's the rush?

If there is one last invitation I have for you, it is to SLOW DOWN, WANT AND NEED LESS MATERIAL THINGS, AND LOVE MORE, for the sake of yourself, the planet and all of us living within it.

The pace we humans are setting ourselves is breaking us, or indeed we are being broken by it.

Action: *Make a list with two columns, one headed 'Wants', the other headed 'Needs' – they will almost certainly present two different lists because what you want and what you need are probably very different. Then ditch some of the wants. Question the list of needs too. Do you in truth need it all?*

Action: *Stop multi-tasking so much. If you have to do this a lot, you are too busy. Give something up!*

Action: *When you are walking, notice the air you are breathing and how your body is functioning for you.*

Question: *Ask yourself, "Why am I rushing so much?", "Where am I in a rush to get to in life?"*

In order to do this work, we really do have to pause first. It's like we have to let the Universe know, without doubt: "I am ready for peace, I am choosing it consciously from my heart and I realise I will have to go through pain thresholds to get there, but I am willing for that for my being and those I come into contact with, including the earth."

We have to slow down generally in order to hear the gentle whispers of the true nature and Integrity of Love. It is not possible for us to hear it otherwise, so if you keep yourself overly busy in your life to distract yourself from your internal pain or so that you don't have to confront what is, then it will not be possible for you to align to the true nature and Integrity of Love. You have to be prepared to sit with yourself in Integrity – Wholeness, Honesty, Non-harmfulness, Unity – and be okay with what you find, while holding a willingness to let go of the darkness. That is being in Integrity. You can then access the true nature of Love that flows through you, but if you do not slow down, you will not be able to open the portal to take you into melding with it.

I also say slow down, because from the perspective of human capacity we are on the verge of explosion. Burnout is rife in western society, with social media and 24/7 accessibility contributing to it enormously. Don't get me wrong, there are some benefits, but the over use and accessibility are where the problems lie.

The irony is that what most people are seeking, the true nature and Integrity of Love, was and has always been available to us. We are just asleep to it or too busy to notice. Humans need to realise the true nature and Integrity of Love has far more benefits than any media platform, and we can actually connect to infinitely more through that. It has so much more power than media on all levels.

Turn off so much of your attention to media and turn it more towards the true nature and Integrity of Love – give yourself this gift.

Get off your phones. If you have taken your child to a school sports day or the weekly cricket practice or you're fortunate to be eating out somewhere or on holiday together – PUT YOUR PHONES DOWN! Get out of your addiction. Just because they are on the cricket pitch does not mean they don't see you are distracted from them. Why not enjoy the fortunate experience in your whole being of witnessing your child's incredibleness as well as your own, while in the presence of the Integrity of Love? They will feel it and you will too. There will be connection that goes far deeper than you taking 20 pictures of what you're eating then posting into the ether, or indeed doing your work emails instead of watching and sharing in the joy of your child's pleasure and abilities or connecting with your partner. Don't allow yourself to deviate and be distracted – discipline your mind in knowing and connecting to the true nature and Integrity of Love in those moments.

If you're out with your dog – be with your dog and don't touch your phone (unless in an emergency, of course). Be with your dog on its walk. Love observing it. Watch how other dogs approaching seem and if they are cautious. Control your dog for its benefit and that of others. Not everyone you pass on a walk will love dogs or want to engage – people have all sorts of things going on behind their exterior – get out of just 'your' world and also consider situations from the perspective of others in your path. Hold compassion for all in mind.

If your child or partner or family member slips their hand or arm into yours – don't simply take it for granted. Notice it. Tell the other what you haven't always told them – don't wait until it's too late. If you've had a row with your partner, forgive them and yourself. Let go of resentment and the need for revenge or to win the battle. Don't blame others, perhaps consider that your past thoughts and actions have caused your current circumstances. Change that, so that you become conscious about your current thoughts and actions. If you need to, get yourself safe.

If you 'hate' someone right now, know that is a very strong word and emotion. It is not helpful to you or the other. Learn to ditch 'hate'. Not one morsel of it has anything to do with the true nature and Integrity of Love. Conquer your anger and this goes from mild irritation to full blown rage and everything in between. It is destructive and again contains nothing of the true nature and Integrity of Love. Swap resistance for acceptance. Neutralise the emotions attached to likes and dislikes and instead be peaceful with what you find. Take responsibility for your actions and don't habitually put the blame on others. Communicate the tough stuff, while holding a space of loving kindness in which to communicate. Consider how your actions will impact on others and discuss it if you think they will find it difficult. If you want to remove yourself from an untenable situation, do so with kindness in your heart. Understand most people are in pain so be compassionate in your actions. Know that you can't help everyone, so if you have tried many options of compassionate behaviours cut your losses and move on, while keeping an open heart allowing the true nature and Integrity of Love to flow through your heart and mind when they come to your attention. Know that you are loved, and the Universe, Buddha, God, Nature, whatever your word for the big stuff is, it has your back and just wants you to connect with the true nature and Integrity of Love.

Question: *Have you ever contemplated that if we stopped producing 'material things' for a year, this planet would have enough to get by and the world would not end?*

What a pause that would be. What an opportunity to invite Love in that would be too. Usually these pauses are brought by war. Only when we are stripped of basics can we experience the true meaning of what matters and that is LOVE. Why should we wait as humans for the next horrific war to teach us what LOVE truly is? Why do you need to lose someone to realise how much you took them for granted and the air that they breathed? Why do people not talk of how many more handbags they wished they'd bought when on their deathbed, but instead they talk of how much they wished they'd forgiven a person or learned how to be more open to Love, Kindness, Peace, and so on. Forget 'things' and grow your understanding of true compassion, true Integrity – Wholeness, Honesty, Unity, Non-harmfulness – the true nature of Integrity of Love and allow its flow; stop blocking it.

SLOW DOWN, WANT AND NEED LESS, LOVE MORE.

Truly sharing Love

As I mentioned at the outset of this book, one of the intentions for it is to share Love. I hope therefore by reading this you feel more inclined and able to connect to the true nature and Integrity of Love and that you will join me in raising awareness for it, so others can heal and purify too, whether that be mentally, emotionally, spiritually or physically.

The more people open into this consciousness, the greater the connection to the true nature and Integrity of Love. We have to be willing to open to it and let it guide us and we can share in this together. Let's do this widely for all.

I hope you have found this book to be beneficial and I sincerely say from deep within my being, I wish you peaceful happiness and that the true nature and Integrity of Love flows through you and round you in abundance. It will if you continue to ask …

What would the true nature and Integrity of Love do?

Part 7: Additional Resources

10 top tips

- Be willing to raise your vibration into awareness and consciousness. Know you are light energy.
- Allow your humanness.
- Slow down, want and need less and Love more.
- Have courage to be deeply honest with yourself and others.
- Hold true compassion at your heart in your actions for yourself and others.
- Listen to others and be present with them, while suspending all judgements.
- Bring in equalness for yourself and for others.
- Know your essence, that of your child/ren and all those around you.
- Come to know that peace is on the inside and connecting with it is an inside job.
- Continually ask, "What would the true nature and Integrity of Love do?" and share that with others.

Resources:

The Integrity of Love
www.theintegrityoflove.com

Jason Garner
www.jasongarner.com

Danu Morrigan
www.daughtersofnarcissisticmothers.com

Kadampa Meditation Centres
www.kadampa.org

Jack Kornfield
www.jackkornfield.com

Caroline Myss
www.myss.com

Further Reading:

Reiki Fire – Walter Lubeck, Frank Arjava Petter and William Lee Rand

Personal Power Through Awareness – Sanaya Roman

Testimony of Light – Helen Greaves

The Four Agreements – Don Miguel Ruiz

Your Body Speaks Your Mind – Debbie Shapiro

Adrenal Fatigue – James L. Wilson

You're Not Crazy It's Your Mother – Danu Morrigan

The Power of Now – Eckhart Tolle

A New Earth – Eckhart Tolle

And I Breathed – Jason Garner

How to Solve Our Human Problems – Geshe Kelsang Gyatso Rinpoche

Love Your Enemies – Sharon Salzberg and Robert Thurman

The Untethered Soul - Michael Singer

The Surrender Experiment – Michael Singer

Notes

Notes

Notes

Notes

Notes

Notes

Notes

Printed in Great Britain
by Amazon

47025290R00109